Carry Eacl

by Paul Gilbert

For all of us.

Published by:
LBC Wise Counsel

ISBN 978-1-8383589-0-7

British Library Cataloguing in
Publication Data available.

Cover picture: Lawrence Smith

I am very grateful for the care, design and
thoughtfulness of Jon Honeyford and Oomph Design for
their work on this and my previous books.

Introduction

In March 2020 the UK followed the rest of the world into lockdown.

Covid 19 has changed the world and the way we work, love and be with each other like no other event in our lifetimes.

As we went into our lockdown in the UK I started to write a weekly blog about the softer needs of leadership, caring for each other and being vulnerable. This book brings together those blogs from March to December 2020 as a weekly memoire of what was on my mind and how I felt we should respond.

Covid 19 has not yet run its course and there may still be dark days to come, but I hope the words I have written will be of some small value and comfort as a quiet reflection on our difficult days.

I hope as well that my words suggest, in our changing world, a kinder, gentler, and more accepting way of just being with each other.

Take care. Paul xx

P.S. I have called this collection Carry Each Other, a sentiment I love and something I have explained further in the penultimate post.

Contents

March 2020:

All will be well in the end, and if it is not well today, then it is not the end...

The last two weeks have been a little disconcerting. We have cancelled our residential events, connecting with delegates and presenters and venues and supporters to offer reassuring messages as best we can. We have seen the majority of clients cancel or postpone activity with us and we have watched our world disappear in plain sight. A vanishing trick that has left us breathless with disbelief.

At times like this being in denial is a pretty cool response.

As a teenager I was once praised for how calm I appeared under pressure, only for the person offering the praise to realise a little later that I had perhaps not fully grasped the gravity of the problem.

In truth however I am seeing things very clearly. The business we have quietly created over twenty years has helped so many, and left a positive mark on careers, teams and organisations. It has done no harm and it has been fun every day. It is more than enough and, whatever is to come, we have been unfathomably lucky.

However the greatest privilege of my professional life has been to work with some of the most extraordinarily talented, kind, thoughtful and inspirational souls anyone could meet. They are woven into the memories we have created and are a constant source of guidance and calm gentleness. They are people who love what they do, and do it with such skill and care that they should never, ever, be out of work for a moment. I love them and love working with them:

Fiona Laird – A wonderful voice coach, full of transformative insights and creator of spellbinding workshops.

Justin Featherstone – The most moving, impactful, skilful and ultimately joyful communicator on leadership I have ever met in my life.

Kay Scorah – Incomparable, joyful, playful and scarily insightful. Kay taught me to listen and I am forever in her debt.

Ciaran Fenton – A uniquely uncompromising approach to helping people who want to be helped. His genius is that he cares that you care.

Hilary Gallo – The best facilitator I know, the best listener I know, the best person to help you move from A to B when you might be stuck somewhere between the two.

Charles Grimes – The man who has worked with us on every LBCambridge programme since 2006 – still the absolute best at what he does.

Jonny Searle – A gifted coach and with joyfully relevant and accessible insights into personal development and leadership.

Claire Lomas – The most engaging and inspiring speaker of her generation.

Martha Leyton and Martin Shovel – The art and the care shine in every moment spent in their company. A communication workshop like no other, but then useful every single day for the rest of our lives.

Richard Martin – The gentlest of men, and someone who will help you curate a positive environment for your personal wellbeing and that of your team.

This is my plea…

If you have some budget now, any budget at all, then please book these people now.

Let them invoice you today and let them know you value their stories, their insights and their ability to change the world for the better. Even if you cannot make a date with them for weeks or months to come, show then you care today. They are the best at what they do, bar none; they are a joy to know and a total privilege to work with.

Please message them.

Show them you care.

Please book them if you can.

Thank you and, as always, please take care.

The least I can do...

It is a time like no other for everyone. We are all grappling with the loss of normality and the shock of sudden change.

I realise, of course, that what I do is not vital to anything and so my loss of normality and my shock at sudden change is unimportant. However, I do have a pretty good sense of what is important; my sister is a palliative care specialist, my niece is a GP and my dear old mum is much loved, but very vulnerable indeed.

I therefore have a very good perspective on what is important, but I want to help, if I can be helpful.

My work is about helping lawyers be the best they can be – to be thoughtful, valued, and inspiring others. Sometimes this means we go like the clappers to get things done, other times we just stand quietly with you as you work things out.

Today, behind the front-line of those looking after all of us, we still need to help all our other institutions and businesses survive and to make their contributions too. We need the lawyers to play their part.

Behind the scenes there is a need for care, thoughtfulness, purposefulness, kindness and brilliant decisions. Behind the scenes there will also be uncertainty, tiredness, and sometimes an almost overwhelming sense of it all being too much.

Sometimes therefore we need a place that is just for us. A place to be heard, to share our concerns, and a place where we can gently place our weary thoughts in the care of someone else for a little while.

This is my email pg@lbcwisecounsel.com and there is no fee to talk with me.

To be honest our accountant has long resigned herself to accepting that we were unintentionally a not-for-profit organisation anyway!

No time limit applies, just put my details somewhere you can find them again if needed. Then, if it might help, please be in touch and we can talk. It is the least I can do, it is also the best I can do.

...a rock, a beach and feeling infinitely small

There is a place in North Pembrokeshire that means the world to me.

A small secluded beach down a narrow lane.

The sort of lane that if you were not sure where you were going, it would convince you with every step that you should turn back.

As if the brambly hedgerows and the overhanging trees jostle you back from where you came.

However, if you keep going, further than you want, a place is revealed that will leave you without a vocabulary to describe how a soul can soar at the sight of something wonderful.

On this beach there is a small, unprepossessing rocky outcrop and within the outcrop it is possible for one person to nestle in a hollowed space so sheltered and secure that peacefulness wraps around you. A peacefulness only matched by a deep sense of belonging to this place in that moment.

Here you can only feel infinitely small and inconsequential.

It is a place to let go of everything noisy that does not matter, and to receive in return something so contemplative and still that it never leaves you even when the noise, inevitably, comes back.

I think about my rock a lot, and I have thought about it even more these last few weeks. It is my place to quell the noise. My place to be secure, to feel infinitely small.

My place to realise that without the noise to accompany them, my worries must be even smaller than me.

No problem is bigger than us, but maybe we need to quell the noise and feel small first to put worries in their place.

April 2020:

This is the time to be slow

...Not everything is an opportunity. Not everyone has time to pause. Sometimes I feel it is too hard to be positive, too frightening to be brave and too uncertain to be strong. The morning breaks and sadness is the first feeling of the day. One day at a time feels daunting enough.

I value and appreciate everyone who can post a kind, hopeful and energetic message, but for me right now I want nothing more than for this to pass and for those I love to be on the other side to work with again, to hold again and to care for again.

I heard BBC Journalist Fergal Keane read a poem the other day and it felt like a good thing to share:

"This is the time to be slow,
Lie low to the wall
Until the bitter weather passes.
Try, as best you can, not to let
The wire brush of doubt
Scrape from your heart
All sense of yourself
And your hesitant light.
If you remain generous,
Time will come good;
And you will find your feet
Again on fresh pastures of promise,
Where the air will be kind
And blushed with beginning."

John O'Donohue, To Bless the Space Between Us: A Book of Blessings

It's not easy, is it?

It's not easy, is it?

I'm afraid I don't have any advice on "ten Tibetan dialects to discover in your new found spare time" or "using Zoom to learn how to knit tank tops from potato peelings" or a "5 step plan to becoming a bookshelf influencer".

I'm just another nobody with a keyboard and an intermediate strength Linked-in profile.

To be honest the first words that enter my conscious mind each morning are "fuck me, oh well, let's put the kettle on". I accept that it lacks the concise majesty of "Keep Calm and Carry On", but if anyone wants to take "fuck me, oh well, let's put the kettle on" as an inspirational slogan for home printed tea towels, please feel free to have it.

However, I don't mean to be flippant either. We all know people who are struggling just now; and one of them might be looking back at you in the mirror. The overwhelming feeling I have every day is that I am helpless to do much, and whatever I do is not enough. It isn't comfortable.

It's not easy, is it?

I welcome the opportunity to clap for carers, I want to be a good citizen, I want to look back with some pride on the way I responded to these extraordinary times. Yet for large parts of each day I feel weighed down by the loss of connection with people I care about, and just plain inadequate when seeing the daily heroic humanity of carers, nurses and doctors.

I don't have school age children and that adds a whole new level of respect and marvel for those who do in these pandemic times. It also makes me feel guilty. How dare I grumble about not being able to have "big" meetings in London, when dear, dear friends have to provide their kids with stimulation, optimism and the strength to carry on, before they themselves have had a chance brush their teeth or give a scintilla of thought to their working-from-home day ahead.

It's not easy, is it?

So, come on Paul, stop feeling sorry for yourself and say something useful.

The problem, however, for me is I know that words alone just bounce off me. You cannot jolly-me-along with a bit of bantz or "interesting" insights if the feelings that have got inside my head don't want me to play with the words.

So, I am not going to pretend to you or to myself that I can jolly anyone along with a few hundred words now. Our feelings win.

However, feelings which take us low must also compete with feelings that bring us back, and we can all help each other create those feelings without any need for a Government press conference to tell us how. And this is the point of these 700 words I am sharing with you now.

We cannot always be clever, or insightful, or heroic. Sometimes we will give up or fail and crack. Sometimes crying is what we must do.

But, ...and it is a big fucking "but" ...WE CAN ALL BE KIND.

Kindness cuts through. Kindness is the smallest noticing of someone else's need. A nod, a wave, a smile, a suggestion, an offer, a thought, a simple acknowledgement, all manner of gentle almost-nothings that make us human and offer a drop of hope for a world where the storm is still swirling.

Thank goodness for heroes, but thank goodness for kindness too. There will always be a need for kindness and there is never a shortage of opportunity to be kind.

We are not invisible when people are kind. We are not alone when we are noticed. We can be in the light that others shine if our light has temporarily dimmed. I love that something that can be so small defines something that is so big. It is far more in reach than discovering Tibetan dialects, and it comes wrapped in the gift of hope.

Making a difference for a lucky few will mean discovering vaccines or designing cheaper ventilators or nursing our loved ones when we cannot be there for them. Making a difference for the lucky many will be the moments of kindness we offer one another, friend or stranger.

It's not easy, is it? But with kindness we give each other hope that we will find our way through.

It is ok to feel a little bit left behind

It is ok to feel a little bit left behind.

Do you remember, back in the day, when people used to have opinions on the quality of coffee they bought each morning, or would ask if you had anything planned for the weekend?

These things are like half-remembered scenes from a docu-drama I might have once watched. An everyday tale of corporate life where episodes revealed the protagonist's preoccupation to be invited to "big" meetings, or to be included on the distribution list for strategic briefings, or to chat casually on the C-Suite floor like they belong. Or perhaps the cliff-hanger episode where they agonise with their boss that "busting my ass for this business feels like a lot more than being fully-fucking-competent, actually…"

This old script looks a little far-fetched to be anyone's reality today, but now we have a different melodrama to cope with, where old stresses are replaced with new ones. New stresses with just one scenic backdrop of long ground-hog days stretching out our already wrought emotions and bending them even more out of shape.

It seems that home-schooling is not a Walton's-esque idyll. Who knew?

Instead it is the metaphorical straw that wrenches the back of every concerned parent each and every day. Except this straw comes in a bloody great big hay bale that has been dropped from a bloody great height and which has smashed everything in sight.

And it seems that working from home is not a charter for the workshy. Who knew?

Instead it is mostly a joyless descent into early evening alcohol as we try to maintain some semblance of giving a damn on back-to-back video calls. It is hard to pretend to be positive or interested in things that were pointless even before this all started. Now these things are pointless on less money with added feral children.

Meanwhile a whole series of space cadets have popped up to invoke either wartime metaphors or wellness tofu.

I do not need wartime rhetoric from politicians straining every sinew to harass people off the beaches; or earnest how-to-do-yoga-in-your-specially-created-mindfulness-room videos from Botox filled influencers who think they are this generation's Vera Lynn – "We'll tint our lashes again some sunny day"

We need competent supply chain management, unrelenting efforts to let science work, kindness all round, and a chance not to feel guilty that we might be feeling a little bit left behind.

I think I can cope with today, but I may not cope with tomorrow. That is it, and it is enough.

I am not giving up, but I am not going to judge myself harshly either. I love the people I love. I care to do the right thing, but I worry about vulnerable relatives, my children's futures, and who gets my credit card statement in my will.

One day at a time.

It is ok to feel a little bit left behind.

And while I am at it, Zoom is witchcraft.

What next then?

...what next then?

Amid much chatter about new normals and paradigms shifting, how will we relate to what happens next? Who to believe and who to follow? I suspect two groups will jostle for the limelight on the starting line.

First, there will be folks who made lots of money before and will not give up their old-world views lightly. They will seek to revert to how things were as quickly as possible. They will be noisy, influential and to be honest they won't always be wrong, but we should be sceptical, and we should ask for more of them. The phrase "elaborate tax saving scheme" is a clue for challenge not celebration.

Secondly there will be the folks who have predicted transformational change from technology, or policy or the end of capitalism for as long as any of us can remember. They may well feel vindicated and relish the spotlight of told-you-so self-regard. If insights emerge about how we move forward, all well and good. However, if what we observe is a self-validating mosh-pit of teenage chimps on a sugar rush, we might need to move on without them.

For most of us however, there will be a quiet yearning to learn something important from all of this, but where that yearning is potentially compromised by our immediate concerns and some crushing worries. Most of us will not have the luxury of time for reflection as we spend months, possibly years trying to rebuild. However, we all still need to find that sense of what truly matters to us in a way that takes away some of the fear and gives us the strength to know that the struggle will be worth it.

To all our leaders therefore I would like to gently offer a few imperfect thoughts.

I suspect your first thought is to get back to work, to drive income and to restore profitability to levels that were anticipated before. I don't mind that. I want you to succeed. However, this is our time to change the way we want leadership to be. We must not waste it.

Please make time to thank everyone. Thank them sincerely and thoughtfully. Thank your teams, your suppliers, your customers. Thank the people you had to let go, and thank the families impacted for all their thoughtfulness too. Thank your lucky stars you can start again. You didn't walk on water before, whatever PR you created around you, and now you know how vulnerable everything can be. Never forget that feeling, but now let's make it better.

Please take a proper amount of time to see what has changed in your business through the eyes of everyone you have just thanked, including and perhaps especially the families. What did we do well and what could we have done better? Apologise for the latter, celebrate the former. Report on it, own it, share it and use it. You have never had a better chance to gather insights like these. It would be such a lost opportunity if the scramble to recreate the old normal meant we trampled over the hopes and fears of people we now need more than ever to help our businesses succeed.

Please re-invent your plans for making a positive and sustainable difference to the various communities you serve. Do not dust off and then whitewash your old CSR policies, but dig deep to make the biggest difference you can. The communities you are part of form an elaborate and beautiful set of intertwined realities, criss-crossing, overlapping and mutually supporting. Please embed your business self-consciously in all the communities you serve and that serve you; leverage their goodwill, support their needs, and build things together.

Please love your people. Love the privilege of employing people in your business. Of course, not everyone works out. Not everyone should be promoted. Some people will sometimes fail; but just as one small example, I would love to think chief executives and all leaders might say something like this in every hiring letter – "We would love you to come and work with us. We want this to be a great experience for you and for us, this may not be the role you want forever, but we want you here with us now; we want to look after your talent so that you are proud to be with us, and we want your commitment and care to make us better".

Please make kindness a measurable and incentivised behaviour. I know share price is important. I know profit and cost-saving are important too. I get it, it goes with your leadership pay grade and leading any business is not easy. However, there is ABSOLUTELY NOTHING in the leadership manual which says that you must be a gigantic, Grade A, bozone emitting, sociopathic, narcissistic knobhead in order to succeed.

Also, and to be clear, being kind is not an excuse for anyone to be sloppy, casual, imprecise, indulged, thoughtless or incompetent.

Being kind is about having fair, transparent boundaries which we all know and observe. It is about respect, it is about high standards and high expectations, but in an environment where we encourage, support and share. If you hire someone who doesn't fit or who doesn't want to buy-in to the values you are living, then there are important decisions to make, but once again you treat people with dignity and respect, with care and concern for their well-being.

I apologise for preaching.

I have no status to judge.

These are just my hopes that for all the pain of loss, uncertainty and hardship so many are experiencing, we will find a better way.

Not everything was wrong before, but I hope we can go forward with fresh eyes to love the difference we can make.

May 2020:

What she said...

Paradigm Shift is not an over-the-counter laxative.

However, I do encourage you to think of it as a highly effective turdilogical expellant next time it is used in an executive briefing paper.

New Normal's alliteration is pretty much all it has going for it. It is utterly meaningless, save that right now there are bedrooms of teenage boys trembling with the thought that "The New Normals" would be a great name for a band. The rise of New Normal however has killed off Sea Change. No-one says Sea Change anymore. It is as if there is a fashion in the latest management bullshit and Sea Change is like Tank Top.

Who wins when language is synthesized into meaningless alliteration for the clickerati?

More importantly, I wonder who loses?

For as long as I have cared about leadership, I have felt excluded from being considered a leader. I am shy, introvert and I dread the sound of my own voice. Neither do I have the energy to care about the latest fashion in management merde-de-jour.

To stand in front of people and share my thoughts on anything felt like the height of implausible self-regard. To assert that I knew best sat so uncomfortably that I could only say things out loud if my words were lagged so tightly in caveats as to be muffled into submission.

I therefore came to accept that the only people who could be leaders were arseholes.

I felt sorry for them at one level, it must be such a burden to go through life being one. Part of me readily understood that this was why they were paid so much. If you can only tolerate the company of people who agree with you, and still be so sensitive to getting your own way, then that must be a terrible curse and the compensation must be in share options. In effect you could only be a leader because you were unemployable in other roles that involved calm, decency, listening, teamwork, kindness and empathy. Thank goodness we had found a way to let them live among us rather than have them locked up.

It is why I have accepted that someone like Donald Trump could be President of the United States. For his type of leadership style, he is the poster child.

He is The Platonic Dick, and I mean that kindly.

These people will always exist, but I think the time has come when we must accept that the social experiment of giving them leadership roles has reached the point when the negative side-effects are outweighing the therapeutic benefits.

For some years now there has been heartening evidence of new leaders coming to the fore. Brilliant people doing brilliant work, and it is a joy to see. Even so, it has also felt that sometimes this new thinking was outside of the mainstream. Pockets of wonder, but still far too much of the old ways. Now however we have a moment in time that we have not had for decades. A time when we no longer have to tolerate old ways that serve only to marginalise concepts of decency, care, community and thoughtfulness just because these values do not fit the caricature of strong, ball-crushing leadership.

As I reach the stage of my working life when I can reflect thoughts with more confidence than I would have dared to say out loud a few years ago, I know there are more and more people who provide the most brilliant examples of what leadership now needs to be. I have been blessed to work with some of them and they are wonderful. I know we will be ok because of them.

I have mentioned Trump, so I must also mention the extraordinary person who said these words:

"One of the criticisms I've faced over the years is that I'm not aggressive enough or assertive enough, or maybe somehow, because I'm empathetic, I'm weak. I totally rebel against that. I refuse to believe that you cannot be both compassionate and strong."

One of the most incredibly heartening things in this desperately sad and unsettling time of our lives, is that we have leaders like Jacinda Ardern to be role models in leadership. Jacinda will encourage others who are already on the same path and inspire so many more to join. I am sure she will have weaknesses and insecurities and have her bad days, but she is also exemplifying how generosity, kindness and care trumps intolerance, self-regard and dogma. What she said will carry me forward.

I am so grateful and so reassured that in my working life I have seen old leadership tropes weaken and diminish, and in their place new leadership values emerge. It isn't certain we will win; we do have to step forward, but we can define leadership our way and we can win.

We can be kind.

Flattening the curve of our emotions

Please forgive this indulgence. A departure from my ranty blogging.

This is a poem I have written to reflect some of the very many mentoring calls I have had in the last few weeks. Most calls start with something inconsequential, but what is sad to hear is when things are said that in normal times would be profoundly difficult, and they are said as if they are inconsequential too.

This poem is just my way of processing some of what I have heard; writing is my way to calm my swirling mind. However what I want to say is that it is ok to be sad when sad things are happening. We must never flatten the curve of our emotions. Please take care. Be kind and never be so alone that you cannot say to someone how you feel. Ranty blogging will return soon.

"How are you?"
"Not too bad. It's a bit strange, but you know – it's ok"

Thank goodness for Wifi
Mustn't grumble, still alive
My boss is great, not demanding
A time to shine while not commuting

"How are you?"
"Not too bad. It's a bit strange, but you know – it's ok"

Home school stuff online is great
Flour's hard to find, weeks to wait
We couldn't say goodbye to dad
Ryanair refund? That's too bad

"How are you?"
"Not too bad. It's a bit strange, but you know – it's ok"

It's nice to sit in the garden though.
No not redundant, just on furlough
Not seen my daughter for weeks
I don't want to read, I cannot sleep.

"How are you?"
"Not too bad. It's a bit strange, but you know – it's ok"

Clapped for all those who are caring
Want to pause when birds are singing
I guess I won't see mum again
Too many runners are a pain.

"How are you?"
"Not too bad. It's a bit strange, but you know – it's ok"

Mustn't cry in front of the kids
Eating what we have in the fridge
So proud of what my colleagues do
I'm not sure anymore, are you?

"How are you?"
"Not too bad. It's a bit strange, but you know – it's ok"

Cheerful on Zoom, but my house is a mess
Virtual drinks help to hide the stress
Not sure if old lives have really gone
The beginning isn't over and the end has not begun.

The courage to be vulnerable and the opportunity to be kind

You have to read the book from the beginning.

You have to watch the film or the TV programme from the beginning too.

If you do not, it will be a significantly poorer experience. There will be gaps and misunderstandings and too many questions. Why would you? It makes no sense. Things make sense when you start at the beginning.

My life did not start at the beginning. Your life did not start at the beginning either. We were all dropped into the plot lines of other people, their stories, their hopes and fears, strengths and weaknesses. Their homes, their families (or not), their towns or cities or villages, their countries. My life is not a film or a book. But the way you see me is as if you joined me on page 179 or scene 23. The way I see you is as if I started watching your story at episode six of series three. It would be a rubbish way to start a book, film or TV series, but it is not a rubbish way to be with you or for you to be with me.

I do not have time to figure out my own story, let alone figure out yours. You cannot make sense of my story and I cannot make sense of yours. But we can choose to be together. We can choose how to be together; and we can choose, when we are together, how to be. Backstories and sequels are for filmmakers, the present is for us.

"Why did you give up being a lawyer?" is a question I am often asked. The proudest day of my professional career, 16 February 1987, was when I qualified. The second proudest day, ten years later, when I became a General Counsel. Then in the year 2000 I ended my career as a lawyer. It had consumed me, terrified me, thrilled me, undermined me and fulfilled me.

Now you know something about me. A glimpse of an earlier plot-line. Would it make our time together any different? No, it would not. If I am kind to you, you will remember my kindness. If I am rude, you will remember my rudeness. If I am dull you will not remember me at all. When I walk into a room, it is not my career that you experience, but how I am with you.

Today the enormity, catastrophe and gravity of our time is impossible to understand. The history of now, only exists in the future. All we can do today is to find the courage to be vulnerable and the opportunity to be kind.

The understandable temptation is to take something that is beyond our understanding and wrap it up in slogans that disguise and deny complexity. The slogans however do not reveal insight, they simply offer a frame for people to argue. A distraction for our ignorance, a denial of our vulnerability, and a missed opportunity to be kind.

As we plan our way out of today and into tomorrow, I hope three thoughts will guide our thinking. If you have any platform at all to lead people and to make decisions on their behalf (whether in government, in business or in communities) may you have the courage to be vulnerable and the opportunity to be kind. For the rest of us, affected by the decisions these people take, then like pieces in a giant jigsaw puzzle, may we be proud of the pictures we collectively create. And finally, for all of us to accept that the scriptwriters for this epic production, do not really exist. We are eight billion human plot-lines, where there is no beginning, and there is no end; there is just now and our time together. A time when we cannot know the whole story, but where this matters so much less when we are kind.

I hope...

The hardest thing will be when it is no longer a crisis and it is just what is left behind.

When flood waters come to a community the flood waters do not come alone. So also come the TV crews with their waders to interview homeowners in their sodden, stinking homes. So will come minor Royalty with a practiced careworn frown and, eventually, will come a Prime Minster swooping by in a bullet proof car, firing off blank promises. When they are gone, what lingers is not a warm glow of care, but broken hopes and the hanging tedium of despair.

In a post lockdown world, the flood of uncertainty and the agony of grief will subside; and what we will be left with will be the biggest challenge of our lives. A challenge where we must try to care and not leave others to despair.

We have built temples to the billionaire gods of market forces on a flood plain of greed, but I hope we will not do so again. I hope that paying taxes will be seen as the privilege of our working lives. Every penny paid creating the wealth to build the legacy of infrastructure for the next generation to come.

I hope we will do more than blindly trust our politicians, caught in their scramble to be popular once every four years, to invest our money in things where the value will only appear long after the expiry date of their careers. Of course we need to build trust in them, but we also need to build a trust fund for our society.

I hope we will embrace the need for an international effort requiring unprecedented levels of contribution, shared risk and cooperation. We cannot socially distance from other nations.

I hope good governance, sustainability, investment, equality, community and fairness will be at the heart of how we judge success. I hope the way we behave towards each other with small acts of everyday kindness, will be valued far more than self-aggrandising gestures of celebrity capitalism.

And I hope, emphatically, we will joyfully accept a collective responsibility to ensure that every life counts.

This is not about trying to build a land of fairy-tales – businesses will sometimes fail, families will sometimes fail, and leadership will sometimes fail too. Life is hard, BUT we can do better.

When we are better with purpose, better with care and better with accountability, then the direction of travel will be good enough. Perfection can wait, today is our commitment to take one better step at a time.

This is not meant to sound like an idealists' charter. A few words on Linked-In are easy, and ideas are cheap, but implementation is key. We have to see that building (and running) a business, creating work and wealth, is an amazing challenge that should be respected and rewarded. However, we must also see that paying tax is the reward for our good fortune, not the punishment.

We must take a collective pride in building our society in the same way that stonemasons took pride in building cathedrals they would never see finished. We must value more the engineers, the scientists, the artists and the thinkers, as well as the millions of doers who keep everything going. We should see the public sector as the foundation for all our protections.

We should ask of everyone, literally everyone, "what can you do, however small, to make this better?"

And for those for whom their illness, infirmity or disability makes this seem impossible, their contribution, vitally, will be to hold those of us who are not yet ill, infirm or disabled to our promise that every life counts.

When the wave of this crisis and the pain of our loss subsides, as it will, we have a chance to build our future. A chance that has not happened for any generation for seventy-five years.

What a time therefore to be alive. What a time to honour the memories of those we have lost and who so sadly cannot share this responsibility with us. Will the grown-ups in the room please stand up, it is our time to lead.

Management theory –
something for the weekend

My first joyful encounter with performance management was the Balanced Score Card. An evolution of the "tick-box" nursery school of management theory. The process required external consultants to describe value and outcomes in such a way that no real roles had any relational context whatsoever to the value or outcomes described.

Management would then observe how colleagues, in the form of an iterative performance dance, would contort their indifference into a sort of management-speak bullshit tango. The charade hung onto its credulity just long enough to hear management's stage-whispered promise that none of it mattered anyway.

Another early encounter with performance management was the Forced Distribution Curve. The theory goes that a representative workforce will have a distribution of performance that maps to the shape of a bell. Most people in this construct sit grumpily in the middle of the bell-curve, with those deemed to be "walk-on-water" wonderful sitting at one end, and others who are deemed to be "sunk-without-trace" sitting at the other end.

It is the responsibility of management to force the performance distribution of their colleagues into one of these three categories: 1) Useless Bellend, 2) Generally Grumpy or 3) Useful Bellend.

The apotheosis of this form of management science was perceived to be the Psychometric Test where, for example, a 17-year-old black-belt 6-Spagma operative, would apply a hideously expensive random letter generator algorithm to literally label 50-year-old employees as under-performing and surplus to need.

This was generally news to all of them as for the last fifteen years their recently retired senior manager, Bob, had always described them as "Outstanding" in formal annual appraisals. Although it appears he had done so largely on the basis that he could not be arsed to fill out the "your journey to personal enrichment" forms and because, as he mentioned in his exit interview, it "fucked with HR's mind".

The only genuinely interesting observable phenomenon when Psychometric Tests are deployed is when a colleague who is a well-known sociopath, is labelled a HPKH (or High Performing Knob Head). In all cases where these letters are given to someone it literally follows like an immutable law of nature that they will be promoted rather than sacked.

On balance I feel we need to have more focus on the human being element of management theory. My personal wish is that we end the jumped-up, self-regarding, dashboard hokum and instead that we focus on three broad concepts.

First, that we set out a clear idea of what we want our humans to do. This will be both in terms of what we hope might be achieved and how we expect our humans to behave towards other humans whatever their rank or role.

Second, that we recruit humans who we believe can do the job and, crucially, we then leave them in peace to get on with doing the job. In all observable tests it seems that if leaders are not dickheads their teams will have fewer dickheads too.

Then third, we ask our humans if they have other needs that we can meet and whether there is anything that we could do better as a result. It might be a long shot, but in this way we might see things improve quietly and organically without the need for the bullshit slurry sprayed over everyone by the HPKH wanting to know if 9:05am is an acceptable time to arrive at the office.

In most instances, the complex organisational paradigm we need for these three outcomes to be predictably achieved is called "The Conversation". However, while this is a reasonably well understood theoretical practice it is often implemented poorly. There will be many instances when it is simply cancelled at short notice, thus leaving the clear impression that the more senior human is after all a HPKH. There will be other times when the more senior human uses up all the allocated time explaining to the junior human how hard it is to be a senior human. Once again this risks the junior human thinking the senior human is a HPKH.

To be truly effective therefore we should aim for an interaction where the more senior human mostly listens to the more junior human. Sadly, this is not rocket science and we cannot therefore give it a fancy name and make HPKH's pay lots of money for an acronym. Thankfully, however it is not rocket science and therefore it requires no budget at all, just an ability to STFU and to show some kindness.

A quiet personal reflection on self-esteem and feeling worthy

It is Mental Health Awareness Week in the UK, and I would like to write something positive and encouraging about mental health and wellbeing.

In 2016 I wrote about being diagnosed with depression. Thankfully it was a relatively light brush with a deeply uncomfortable illness. With love and support I recovered well and believe I have learned to manage the odd dip since.

I do not feel my depression has gone forever, but I now have a perspective on it that gives me hope it will not overwhelm me again. Partly for me this has been about acknowledging that my vulnerability should not be hidden. I do not think we can pretend to be invulnerable and cope well forever. I have found that it is better to accept vulnerability as part of the mosaic of our lives and to let it make the picture so much more vivid and real.

In this blog therefore I would like to share a little about self-esteem and self-worth. I know when anyone is struggling it is easy to think that everyone else is coping brilliantly. Our weaknesses make us feel very lonely. I hope therefore that it might be helpful to someone if I write a few words about the fact that I have never coped brilliantly with, or indeed felt worthy of, any role I have ever had.

I have heard people say lots of kind things over the years; they say I can be an inspiring speaker and sometimes a funny writer and some people think I am an insightful mentor. Such kind words are appreciated and I count my blessings every day, but it is not the same as what I feel.

As a director of the business I founded in the year 2000 I have worked all over the world from Singapore to Cape Town to Washington. However, I am certain there has not been a single day when I felt worthy of the opportunities I have been given.

In twenty years I have not been able to accept even one compliment without an overwhelming wish to say back "yes, but you're wrong..."

How can it be that in my late fifties I have so little regard for my experience that I still feel gripped with anxiety before a presentation?

I have been part of a team that has created wonderfully enriching developmental events, but I do not sleep for days beforehand and afterwards I struggle to read the often beautifully thoughtful feedback from a grateful delegate.

I love my mentoring work. The people I work with are gifted and kind, and they inspire me with their courage, and their commitment to being thoughtful and brilliant contributors. To help such brilliant people fulfil their potential feels like one of the greatest blessings of my life, but I have never asked any of them if I have helped.

I love writing, but I would be mortified to have my words critiqued. I write mostly to calm my swirling mind and so that my exhausted ideas may rest away from the noise inside my head. I was once told by a lawyer that he was disappointed with a report I had written. "Is this it?" he asked before destroying my work. He concluded his email saying, "You know you are not as good as you think you are". I thought to myself "Mate, you have absolutely NO idea!". The email is years old and it is still the only feedback I can remember word for word. And the trouble was, I believed him.

My self-doubt is part of me. On a good day I can appear like I have it all under control, I can trust that I have done things before and I will therefore be able to do these things again. But on a poor day I doubt I will ever work again.

The reason I feel it is important to share this most private of fears, in this Mental Health Awareness Week, is because it is also the twentieth anniversary year of our business and I want to say out loud, proudly and with certainty that my fear has not defined me.

My fear has not stopped me from being a contributor and helping other people. My fear has not stopped me from being valued by others. My fear has not stopped me from trying to be kind.

There are a few things at the heart of the way I work, and I would like to share them with you. I think they are the most important things I have learnt in my whole career and without these thoughts I would have been lost a long time ago.

First, if you feel that you cannot love yourself you must still allow others to love you. I know I am not the best judge of my worth, but I trust others who love me to guide me and help me.

Second, if you cannot easily ask for help, please surround yourself with people who will step in to help you without being asked. The best teams look out for each other. The people I work with inspire me every day. The people around me have changed my life for the better, for ever.

And third, if you fear a bad day is closing in, try to let it pass, a good day will not be far behind. Your talent and your values are a constant, a stormy mind is not. In the hauntingly beautiful words of John O'Donohue:

"This is the time to be slow,
Lie low to the wall
Until the bitter weather passes.
Try, as best you can, not to let
The wire brush of doubt
Scrape from your heart
All sense of yourself
And your hesitant light.
If you remain generous,
Time will come good;
And you will find your feet
Again on fresh pastures of promise,
Where the air will be kind
And blushed with beginning."

Whatever our fear, however it feels, it emphatically does not define us. Fear may want to engulf us, but it cannot do so. It is just one feeling, and we have so many others to rely on. Fear can shout and make a din, but noise is not the same as truth. Despite my fear, which I have had for as long as I can remember, I know it is possible to have a career full of blessings, full of achievement, full of love and kindness and friendships for a lifetime. That is the truth.

Perhaps it is because of my fear that I have found the most beautiful and cherished people to work with; people full of soul and kindness. Perhaps it is because of my fear that I know there is such untapped potential in everyone, and I believe in everyone's opportunity to be the wonderfully kind, thoughtful and fulfilled contributor that they and their talent deserve to be. Perhaps it is because of my fear that I feel it is my life's work to stand beside others and their fears.

My final thought is for my colleagues at LBC Wise Counsel and in our amazing faculty. I love working with you. I love your kindness and your brilliance. I love the values you live by every day. I love you. You have lifted my world and filled it with blessings. Thank you.

Be more Crumble – lessons in leadership

Crumble is not a lawyer.

She is not "C-Suite experienced".

Neither is she a "dynamic, commercial, self-starting Executive with a track-record of transformational achievement".

She is a four-year old cockerpoo. Her daily routine is simple and pretty much the same every day. She wakes up, has a wee in the back garden, has breakfast, naps, goes for a walk, naps, goes for a wee in the back garden, naps, has supper, goes for a walk, naps, goes for a wee in the back garden and goes to bed.

In four years however I have learnt more about leadership from her than any chief executive I have ever worked with.

My friend, and one of the most brilliant and important commentators on leadership in Britain today, Ciaran Fenton, would observe how Crumble passionately adheres to the "Feel – Need – Do" model. She expresses her feelings precisely, with a clear, simple communication strategy. She is always specific about her needs. There is no fudging, no ambiguity nor any dissembling. And she always follows up with actions that respect her needs and feelings.

Her "EQ", as Ciaran would observe pithily, is "through the roof – one-hundred feckin' percent!"

Another dear friend, Kay Scorah, noted with me recently how lockdown had given more space for emotions to be felt and noticed. In the same way we have all noticed birdsong without the noise of traffic, so in a stripped back world, we are perhaps a little more conscious of how we feel.

Kay's work in this area of building empathy, and therefore of building understanding and consensus through an awareness of what is happening in the moment, is both beautiful and profound. To be successful leaders must be able to share emotion and be aware of the emotions of others. Not to be needy, but to be authentic. Not to overwhelm others, but to be truly present with them.

Crumble has an extraordinary capacity to always stay in the moment – whatever has passed, whatever is to come she will be with you, stay with you and allow you to be your true self.

I am privileged to regularly work with and admire one of the most empowering presenters I have ever heard on leadership theory. He is Justin Featherstone MC and to be with this humble, gentle and softly spoken man is part of the realisation that leadership is all about caring for others. Caring so that others may be the best version of themselves they can be on any given day in any given situation. In his work Justin emphasises how leadership is being part of the team (not apart) and how fitting in, being generous, kind and loving matter, even in the seemingly brutalising environments in which soldiers work.

Caring for others should be a visceral experience not something synthesised into slogans.

To see Crumble effortlessly look after the emotional needs of her pack, fitting in, being generous and unconditional in her affection, is in its small way humbling too. She asks for nothing except the opportunity to be her best with you.

Ray Berg is the Managing Partner of Osborne Clarke. Ray and his colleagues have been a wonderful source of encouragement support for our programmes, and personally to me too. In many respects he offers a leadership style that draws on all these things I have mentioned already, but he is also more than these things. Ray is generous and kind and thoughtful, but he is also his own man, authentic and vulnerable. He has not mimicked anyone but has not been selfish either.

There is also one other thing to observe, Ray is constantly exploring boundaries and challenging accepted norms, but never grumpily if it does not happen at first.

In her way too Crumble with a lightness of touch and a glint in her eye will push at all accepted norms (mostly around where she can sleep and what she can eat) but never with anything other than a gentleness that is in the end harder to resist than if she growled her way through the day.

My final leadership lesson from Crumble is also exemplified by another of our wonderful faculty who we have the privilege to work with and call a friend. Fiona Laird is a theatre director, voice coach, artist, writer and musician. She has a phenomenal expertise and works with extraordinarily gifted people who are at the very top of their worlds, and yet she is also generous and kind to everyone who asks for her help.

Delegates who come to our programmes are perhaps unlikely to also appear at the National Theatre or at the RSC, but Fiona will give each of them the same care as she would a significant acting talent.

To wear your expertise so lightly, but to honour it so profoundly is the mark of a beautiful leader.

Crumble also has a phenomenal expertise. Her nose is one of nature's most accurate and complex sniffing devices. Crumble has gifts we cannot imagine, but she will use her gifts every day and in every situation. What a wonderful thing to be so devoid of ego and selfishness that the gifts one could bring to the world are offered to it so unconditionally.

In my life every day I try to be more like Ciaran, to be more like Kay, and Justin and Ray. I hope to aspire to be more like Fiona too, and of course to be more like Crumble.

We should all be more Crumble.

A love letter, not a flag of convenience

The most important space between us is not a physical distance, but how closely we are prepared to align our vulnerabilities.

To embrace an idea shared with us, is to be vulnerable with our thoughts. To trust someone, is to be vulnerable with our heart. To care about something is to be vulnerable with our time. We could be a thousand miles apart, but totally and joyfully inseparable.

The words we use, the time we share, the kindness we show and the space we allow for others to be heard, are like the individual stitches in the fabric of a relationship. They bring us together and then hold us together. The physical distance between people is then no gap at all.

The most important aspect of leadership is not the cleverness of the strategy, or the smartness of the rhetoric. Neither is it the status or the power seemingly conferred by hierarchy. Leadership is about how we align and respect vulnerability. Can I make you feel that I am worthy of your ideas? Can I make you feel that I am worthy of taking you away from your family to give me time? Can I make you feel that I am worthy of your trust?

Leadership is too often painted as a sweeping landscape of populism and soaring tones. In reality it is pixels of care and thoughtfulness.

The wonderful irony in our current separateness, is that we can feel more connected than ever before because of the kindness and thoughtfulness we show each other.

In our recent history we have built gleaming towers to house the egos of our leaders. They are statements of status and exclusiveness. Their call to prayer is to shout, "fuck you world, look how we gleam all over your inconsequence". Now these towers are empty, hollow and without purpose. We no longer bustle past besuited avatars and crowd into lifts packed with people, but seeing no-one. Instead, despite the variable quality of our Wi-Fi, we see real people in real homes.

We notice small things and we care more that people are ok.

Leadership has been a flag of convenience for driving income and beating the competition; my wish is that it becomes a love letter to our people and our communities.

As we start the process of returning to what we thought was normal, we must ask more of our leaders. We are, after all, the reason others can be leaders. We must still be profitable and we must be competent. There will also always be boundaries, as there are in all loving relationships, but our opportunity is to reset what leadership means.

Leadership is in the stitching together of our interests in common, a patchwork of vulnerable humanity, made strong by our values and shared endeavour.

Leadership is to facilitate our growth as contributors, not as takers.

Leadership is to care about the smallness of our human needs, not the implausible grandness of our corporate ambition.

Living in colour

Have you been moved by music, nestled in its hold, made humble by the beauty of sound? Have you cried in a film or at a play when words have brushed against your unseen hopes and fears? Has a photograph made you laugh out loud, or brought a silent tear? Have you connected so completely to a sense of time and place that by remembering it, you will never be truly lost again? Have you stood in silent wonder? Have you received kindness? Have you been made to feel that you are worthwhile? Does someone make you feel special? Do you make someone feel special? Do you believe in your soulfulness?

How do you measure any of this? What metric is there for the things that move us?

The more I think about the world of work, the more I have a sense of its tendency to diminish us rather than to build us up. We live in a world of vivid colours, but where work is all too often monotone and dull.

Back in the last century I once had a proper job. I was a young lawyer in a suit that was smarter than my contribution, anxious to find a way to be comfortable with my life choices. One afternoon I was in my boss's office, it was appraisal time. "What do you want to do next?" he asked me... And I said something about "Well, I would like to manage a team some day?"

"Why?" he asked, with more than a hint of "yeah, sure?".

My answer was as hesitant as my confidence, and I stumbled into sentences like a drunk man navigating a room full of chairs. What I tried to say was this, "I don't want to be in charge, or to tell people what to do, I am not bothered by grade or job title, but I do not want people to feel like I do when I come to work."

A year or two later I was managing a team, and even as I write those words I am struck by the absurdity of the language.

"Managing a team" is meaningless in its familiarity. It is just another unsophisticated synthetic dilution of what is in truth a simple act of being with people, caring about people, and helping people. Is it any wonder that for some, managing a team is not about people, but an inconvenient imposition on their time, the compensation for which is an additional line on their CV.

Back in that appraisal meeting so many years ago, I can still feel the uncertainty and discomfort of my younger self, but I also see that I was on to something. In the years that followed I have been blessed to learn from others who have touched my life with indelible kindness and moments of truth.

It perhaps risks trivialising meaning to mention specific moments, but I want to show you what I feel.

Few people sit with me better that Hilary Gallo sits with me. To sit with someone is such a generous act. To be still in another's presence is to honour whatever might be said next and it is such a gift.

No one asks me how I am feeling with more kindness than Richard Martin. The pause he offers after the question is a place for honesty not superficiality.

To know that being a good person does not make anyone immune from ethical pressure is a thought I reflect on every day and owe to Richard Moorhead. As I do his need to challenge kindly, but with rigour and purpose if we want things to be better.

To see Martin Shovel and Martha Leyton working with the most sophisticated minds, but asking them to play with the power of words they learnt when they were four years old, is a revelation of communication.

To watch John Sutherland quietly deconstruct the most complex economic or corporate puzzle is to be invited to sit next to a master of his art. And in a world that until I met John, I always felt excluded people like me.

Charles Grimes is the best in the world at what he does, but he asks nothing of me except the opportunity to work together again. How could you not love that thought?

To see Jonny Searle lean into a conversation to explore an idea, is to realise that humility sits most comfortably with those for whom achievement has always been a shared endeavour.

And then to observe the way Carolyn Kirby, who with so many extraordinary and unique life achievements, ignores the free-wheel to an easy chair. Instead each day she brings positivity and selfless duty to the causes and people that mean so much to her. Leadership as a privilege, not for the privileged.

They have shown me how leadership is a tapestry of thoughtfulness, an infinite story of small acts that are both personal and universal, specific to me, but also for everyone.

In my life they have made leadership as vivid as the music, films, plays and photographs that have moved me. They are my sense of time and place when I pause to wonder what leadership means. They have offered me the key to a treasure trove of ideas and values that are now mine to explore and use. They have given me moments that have touched my soul and I now see leadership in colours of kindness and care, not in the monotone soullessness of process and superficial theory.

I urge you to find your palate of vivid colours in the people around you so that you can shine your brightest and lead in your true colours.

June 2020

I don't want to be a bystander anymore

A few months ago, I was looking forward to June and the pleasure of two or three pleasant evenings at the cricket after a busy day of work. Pints of ale with friends and my all too predictable conversation about how Test Matches are so much better than the T20 format of my favourite sport.

It is the perfect inconsequential relaxation. A privileged man with a pint and an opinion, in a benign and trivial environment; a sort of safe play area to leave me while the world gets on with its chores.

FYI, I have a few predictable conversations. I have never understood why people put on Lycra and run for fun. Honestly, just leave a little earlier, wear looser clothing and smile more. I would also ban salad. Food that is mostly cold, limp and wet has absolutely nothing to endear it to me. It is the food of last resort in any fridge of substance, and I believe restaurants only use it to inhibit our carbohydrate guilt.

Part of me wishes for a world where it was still ok to be so exercised by such small things, a world that used to make space for my vacuous banality and my privilege. The problem is that a world making space for my privilege also made space for too many others to live with unimaginable prejudice and pain.

It has brought me up short.

In recent weeks I have written a lot about kindness and love and caring. I have spoken about the power of seemingly small kind acts, because in a world where we seem not to have power over our lives, we always have the power to be kind. We do not need a budget, or a job title or permission to care.

There is however another feeling; a feeling which questions what use is kindness if a dear relative has died alone in a care home, or if you are a black man with a policeman's knee on your neck?

So, let me put a little edge on how empowered we are, even now.

In fact, how empowered we are especially now. I know I am privileged, but knowledge not ignorance is the privilege I want to claim for my life's chances.

I will not therefore outsource my integrity and let the inadequacy of leaders be a proxy for my subsequent excuses. I am not a bystander in what happens around me, I am a participant.

The issues our world faces are easy to see, but I know I have found it easy to walk by muttering it is not my job and it is definitely above my pay grade. However, I want to frame things differently. It is not my job to recruit, train and lead police officers in the United States. However, I can educate myself on historical injustices and know how this seeps into the structural inequality of today. It is not my job to invent the Covid-19 vaccine. However, I can contribute to slowing down the risk of infection in the short term, while scientists seek to protect me in the long term. It is not my job to make the tax system fairer, or to design policies that help us meet our climate change imperatives. However, I can have an opinion and I can share what I think with colleagues, friends and family.

It is not hopeless, but hope alone is not a strategy. Leaders may have the privilege of power, but you and I have the power of influence. In this moment when things are frankly awful, I must not assume someone else, somewhere else, must be doing something. I must decide that I can do something, however small it might seem, and I must act.

I therefore make these promises. First, I will not outsource my integrity to others. I will ask more of those who have been gifted the privilege of influence over my life. I will say "not in my name" when my silence might be taken as permission by those who should know better. Second, I will offer kindness because I know it touches people and stays with them forever. I can also amplify the cause of others and offer them love and care for their needs.

When the lockdown began, I said that if anyone needed to talk, then my mentoring work would be free of charge. So far, I have shared more than 150 hours with extraordinary people from New Zealand to

New York, from all backgrounds and all parts of the legal profession. I am so grateful for the structure and purpose this has given this period of my uncertainty. It has been a gift to me. Now, if law firms or in-house teams would like to work with me to offer mentoring support for colleagues starting out on their careers and who come from traditionally excluded backgrounds, I will gladly offer my time for free for as long as it is helpful. It isn't much, but I don't want to be a bystander anymore.

Are you good at change?

Are you good at change?

Comfortable with change?

Or are you change resistant?

Don't people bang on about change?

Nothing should change.

Everything should change.

Something should change.

But what should change?

What should not change?

What is enough change?

Hardly changed?

How should the change you make, change the things that are to be changed?

If things are not changed, are they still changed by other things changing around them?

What if change is not a thing, but an idea, or a feeling or a behaviour?

What if we do not all change together at the same time?

Have we ever all changed together at the same time?

What should happen if some of us want change, but others do not?

If you want to change something, are you changed if you are not allowed to change?

Can I impose my change?

Do I accept change imposed on me?

Do we need a changing room?

What about loose change?

You've changed, haven't you?

You haven't changed a bit, or have you?

Change is a metaphor.

Unless something is actually changed, then it can be a real change and a metaphor.

Or just a real change and not a metaphor.

If change is a constant, is that change?

The only thing that changes is the excuse we use for not changing.

Have you changed your mind about change?

Change is how we grow, unless it makes us smaller.

Change the record, the nappy, the seasons, the tune.

Can we change places.

If I were you or if you were me...
...would we see change differently?

Some thoughts on mentoring in lockdown

At the end of March 2020, the UK finally went into a formal lockdown. Schools closed, offices emptied, and the skies were left for the birds.

Linked-in filled up with a thousand optimistic ways to make working from home an Instagram-able tableau – a sort of workstations of the crass; while Twitter just carried on as before, lashed to brown-water log flumes carried down effluent filled rabbit holes.

Lockdown began like a scene from a post war film where Trevor Howard might have said to Celia Johnson in perfectly clipped calmness "Yes my dahling, we have no schools and no loo rolls, but we have our furlough and an undimmed spirit to overcome this despicable johnny virus. Let me light your cigarette in this dimly lit carriage so that our eyes alone convey just how much our love of the NHS surpasses that for our own inconsequential lives".

However, the romanticism did not last long, soon we were thrown down the laundry shoot into a dystopian scene from our own hellish imaginations. Here was the raw reality of elasticated waists, dunking digestive biscuits in gin and flicking the crumbs into yesterday's casually discarded yogurt pots. Meanwhile the older children swapped long division and French adverbs for filming their two-year old sibling pour baked-beans over the family cat.

I do not mean to make light of all this. In fact I want to be very serious.

I have mentored lawyers for twenty years and have a good sense of their pressure points as well as their opportunity to feel more fulfilled. It was obvious that lockdown would test us all, and when I offered to listen, I knew it was important for people to feel heard. I can now share some of the predominant themes that have emerged over the last three months of listening. If these themes resonate with you, I hope that knowing they are shared might make our fears, disappointments and anxieties weigh just a fraction lighter.

Isolation:

Working from home for many people is neither ideal nor idyllic. However superfast the connectivity, social connection matters even more; including all those incidental and seemingly inconsequential moments of unplanned conversation. The social network is our gently woven safety net for sharing and receiving clues about our confidence, comfort and wellbeing. Moments that offer miniature safety valves for us to release our cares, and moments that offer the places where we can leave and collect our mood clues.

These moments not only make us feel human, they help us perform better. Instead we are sheathed in layers of digital filters which diminish the experience of engaging and enhance our anxiety at the same time.

What is of even more concern is to hear how some people are being subjected to an incessant drip, drip, drip of coercive bullying. The layering of our guilt upon our undermined confidence is such an insidious combination. Without our usual outlets to share and care, we are alone. Horribly alone.

Leadership in this context cannot be just a jolly all hands check-in to see newly lipsticked smiles and palm-tree virtual backgrounds; it is to call people up, and to listen. It is to say we expect less and that we will support more. It is to know what invisible connections have been lost and to find ways to compensate for them.

Exhaustion:

Tiredness comes in different forms. There is the tiredness from exertion; the tiredness of not sleeping so well and the tiredness of convalescence. There is however a terrible tiredness that falls on those who feel alone and without hope for a solution. If we know the dawn will come, we will cope with the darkness; but if we doubt the light will ever return, every moment in the dark is almost unbearable. My sense right now is that so many of us are simply exhausted. Worn down and reduced in ways that are both profound and sad.

Leaders must understand how serious this feeling is becoming for far too many people. Leaders must not make assumptions that just because we are all a bit fed up with queuing at Asda, and not being able to hug a relative, that somehow, we just have to cope. This is not about mild inconvenience and needing a nap, this is a visceral exhaustion that is making people feel ill.

Things will not be the same again, ever:
It is true that even in the best of times none of us know what will happen in the future.

A predictable future does not exist for any of us, but before lockdown some of our futures felt more predictable, more within reach. Right now, the uncertainty we feel for what might be next and how the coming years will unfold is palpable. Will we have work? Will we be able to travel? Do our children have the same opportunity to be happy? Will we see live music again? Will we dance in crowded rooms?

The sense of not knowing means we are relying on hoping, and hope is a very vulnerable and very dependent narrative.

There comes with this feeling a sense of loss as well. A lost expectation and a loss of control. We are mostly creatures of habit. We signpost our lives with predictable moments of affirming and re-enforcing emotional re-charging. A sense of renewal, where hope and expectation hold hands on our familiar and well-trodden pathways.

Leadership now is about understanding how this feeling plays out for people. The kindest thing to do, might just be to sit with someone.

I will finish with a sense of my reflections at this time. You do not have to be elderly to feel isolated. You do not have to work in an Intensive Care Unit to feel exhausted and you do not have to be depressed to feel hopelessness. We should not feel guilty just because we are not heroes. We should not dismiss our feelings because some others are bound to be worse off than us. We must not be supervised as if we cannot be trusted and we must not be bullied because we are less visible and less connected to our supportive colleagues and friends.

This is fucking hard. We are not machines.

Look out for each other. Look after each other.

Be kind to yourself. Be kind to each other.

The parable of the schoolboy General Counsel

"Pick it up" said the teacher, exasperation furrowing her brow and losing patience through every pore of her being, like boiling cabbage water draining from a colander.

"But it wasn't me Miss" said the little schoolboy again, the injustice burning a small blister of indignation on his innocent mind and hurting more than any physical pain.

"I don't care" said the teacher, "it does not belong on the floor and I have now asked you five times to pick it up".

"Four times Mi…" the word was not finished before a howl of anger overwhelmed the little boy…

"ENOUGH-PICKITUP-NOW!"

…And so begins the parable of the schoolboy General Counsel.

The little schoolboy General Counsel always knew he had five groups of people to please. He must serve the head-teacher and her staff. He must not let the school down and wear the uniform with pride. He must be part of his class and play nicely. He wants his family to be proud of him and he wants to fit in with his General Counsel friends who go to different schools.

He also knew there was something else. Something in the background. Not everyone was called General Counsel. He wasn't sure what it meant as descriptions were vague and only existed in partial stories handed down at gatherings of other General Counsel. He wasn't allowed to go to these gatherings however because they usually fell on school days.

He did half remember one story. A story about a book of regulation that no one had seen or read. A book with a secret page about General Counsel. A page that spoke of higher duties and special rules. The story gave him a feeling that he was special, but without the detail he could not say why he was special or what it might mean. However, he noticed that General Counsel seemed not to care about the rules and simply relied on asserting exceptionalism to carry them through their school days.

Then one day, an older boy, no longer in school asked him directly about the secret page in the book of regulation that no one had seen or read.

"Why are you asking me?" shuffled the little schoolboy General Counsel "And who are you anyway?"

"I used to be a schoolboy General Counsel" said the older boy, calmly but with some sadness in his eyes. "In fact, I was here in this school, just like you."

"What happened?" asked the little schoolboy General Counsel.

"I wanted to please everyone. I wanted to fit in; to be the teacher's pet, and best friends with the cool kids, and accepted by the edgy kids, and not hated by the bad kids. I wanted to win the school cups and to beat the other schools when we played them. I loved the acceptance and needed more." The older boy's tone was almost wistful, like he was explaining things to himself.

"What's wrong with that?" said the schoolboy General Counsel, "That sounds perfect to me!"

"That's the problem" said the older boy, "...it isn't ever perfect. We try to please five groups, but without the secret page in the book of regulation that no one has seen or read, we are not General Counsel."

"What does it say?" asked the little schoolboy General Counsel.

The older boy leaned forward and spoke softly, but firmly, "The words mean nothing, and they mean everything. They are not remembered because they have not been read. They are not enlightening because we prefer the dark. The words do not provide direction, because instead we trust the people we want to please to know the way. We deny the value of the words because they add nothing to our fun. We ignore them because we are told by others that we are special. We diminish them because we tell ourselves we are exceptional. We do not challenge their meaning because we have grown comfortable with pleasing people instead. We accept compliments without challenge, awards with entitlement and winning becomes our reason to be."

"I don't understand" said the little boy General Counsel.

"You are not special or exceptional" said the older boy. Do not infuse being a General Counsel with those thoughts; but as a General Counsel you must know the secret page in the book of regulation. It is the only reason you can be here.

"You still haven't told me why you left the school" the schoolboy General Counsel asked again...

The older boy looked down and took from his pocket a crumpled scrap of paper. As he smoothed the paper out on his knee, he started to speak...

"A teacher shouted at me once. She said I had to pick something up that others had left. It was a terrible mess. She wanted me to tidy it way like it had never happened. It was not my fault, but I saw the other boys who made the mess and I knew who they were. I didn't tell the teacher who they were. So now I had to clear up the mess. It was not my fault. I cleared it away like nothing had happened. I cleared away the mess as if it was my mess. And now it was, always and forever, my mess too. The teachers thought I was silly, my family did not understand, the other boys didn't like me anymore and I could not share with the other General Counsel in case they laughed at me behind their awards. The school was not the same again. I needed to leave, I had to leave."

The older boy then paused to give the little schoolboy General Counsel the now smoothed out scrap of paper and he pressed it into his hands.

"Please do not let these words be a secret to you ever again".

Leadership now – 30 brief thoughts to share:

What should we require of our leaders in a post-pandemic professional services business?

In this note I share my thoughts on what I hope leadership can mean at this time, of all times.

These thoughts are based on twenty years of working with the most extraordinary people at all levels in the organisations that I have been lucky enough to serve.

From change projects, to mentoring, to training current and future leaders, I have had the privilege of working all over the world, from Singapore to Johannesburg, and in cities across Europe and North America too. I have seen brilliance and I have witnessed failure. All leaders come and go, but the mark they leave, good or bad, will stay in the memories of those they influence forever.

In a post-pandemic world, leaders have an even bigger responsibility than ever before to do the right thing and to do it well. In this very brief note, I share only the headline thoughts of what I know will be required. The detail is for each leader to create and to embrace.

What to measure:

1. Measure the difference people make and compare this to the difference you asked them to make.
2. Measure integrity
3. Measure kindness
4. Measure the impact of your leadership on your employees, employee families, shareholders, customers, suppliers and the communities in which you do business.
5. Measure how sustainable your activity is and plan to improve sustainability further.

How to lead:

6. Be vulnerable, be kind and be clear. Narrate your thinking and invite opinions before you decide things, not to support what you have already decided.

7. Engage continuously and thoughtfully with employees, employee families, shareholders, customers, suppliers and the communities in which you do business.

8. Listen and always acknowledge what you have heard.

9. Highlight your mistakes.

10. Be alive to the possibility of group thinking, and therefore encourage constant challenge, as long as the challenge is in line with the values of your culture.

11. Celebrate the success of how things were achieved, not just what has been achieved.

12. Congratulate your competitors when they do well.

13. Sit with people more, not to share your thoughts or to be validated yourself, but just sit with them to listen.

Practical steps:

14. Recruit people who exemplify your values and who will help you to build the culture you are creating. Experience and expertise matter of course, but nothing matters more than the values of the people you hire.

15. Where people work matters, whether this is at home or in the office. Therefore, care about their home life, care about their office life, and care about what being part of a team means for them and for you.

16. Invest in the development of potential in all your people at all levels of your organisation. Treat all colleagues (whether interim, temporary, part-time, or permanent) the same. They are not columns on a spreadsheet, but people.

17. Invest in the communities in which you trade – not for headlines, or photo opportunities, but for the difference you can make to the lives of people who live around us.

18. Do not tolerate behaviours that undermine your values.
19. Be explicit about the things that matter and align all rewards with the things that matter
20. Abandon any plan that compromises your values and be as vocal about your actions to stop bad things as much as you are to create good things.
21. Remove any requirement for minimum hours or maximum holiday. Trust your recruitment, trust your values and trust your culture to get the job done.

Change the narrative of success:

22. Your job is to hand over to your successor a kinder, healthier, happier business.
23. Your job is not too maximise income as an end in itself.
24. Your job is not drive out costs as an end in itself.
25. Your job is to create an environment in which people can thrive in a sustainable way that supports family life and enhances communities.
26. Pay your taxes and celebrate how much you pay.
27. Protect what matters, and challenge anything that is destructive of what matters.
28. Invest in projects that you personally will never see the value from in your tenure as leader. Pay forward for others to know you cared.
29. Be proud of the way you behave.
30. Leave as friends.

And, within all this, leaders must of course champion pay equality, embrace the Black Lives Matter movement, honour diversity in all its forms and unlock potential wherever it can be found. I want every leader to say, "on my watch these things improved".

The world of work was never just an economic construct. Leadership should never be judged on financial metrics or incentives alone. In the end leadership is the privilege to influence lives; we should relish the opportunity this privilege provides.

A letter to General Counsel about being in the room

Dear General Counsel,

Please forgive my impertinence in writing to you this evening.

I would like to draw your attention to a report by Professor Stephen Mayson entitled "Reforming Legal Services Regulation – Beyond the echo chamber."

Professor Mayson's report is an extraordinary endeavour and commendable for many reasons. It has been meticulously researched, it is comprehensive and very accessible. It marks a point in time of great change for our country and notes the significant and constant change in the legal profession. I commend it to you if you care at all about our profession and its standing in our society.

I will not comment in this letter on the wider implications of the changes we see today, but I do want to comment on your world.

I am, and always have been, someone who cares deeply for the world you work in. The world of the in-house lawyer. If you do nothing else with the report please read the section that applies directly to you, from Page 147.

Let me be clear, I am not advocating that in-house lawyers should be subject to new or additional regulation. In part this is because I do not believe the SRA or the Law Society have an appetite at this time for further regulation. In part I suspect you do not think it is necessary either.

The SRA, the Law Society and you might be right, but you might not be.

I do not ask you to justify your views, but I do ask you to reflect as a leader in our great profession on what it means to be a lawyer today. What does it mean in your world to act with integrity, with independence, in the client's best interests and to uphold the rule of law and the administration of justice?

In your reflections would you please ask of yourself to search answers to these questions:

What are the transparent and accountable competencies needed to be appointed to the role of General Counsel? Are there any minimum qualifying competencies or qualifying experience or qualifications needed? Should not one of the great offices of corporate governance have a meaningful qualifying standard?

How would you judge your independence? How would anyone else judge your independence? What accountability do you owe to the owners of your business to act independently?

In what sense do you uphold the rule of law and the administration of justice. When your company comes under the most intense scrutiny or threat, at what stage does expedient governance become something that is permissible on your watch?

How do you know that your amazing colleagues share your view of how to interpret the cherished principles of being a lawyer?

In a world that has been tipped upside down, how do your ethical boundaries guide you? How would we know?

I do not mean for any of this to sound like criticism. The view from the boundary is not the same as facing the bowler. You have my respect. However, it is because I care about you that I ask these questions. It is because I care about you that I would like you to feel supported by our regulatory frame and not inconvenienced by it.

I have five suggestions I would like you to consider. None of them are about more regulation for you or your team or your business:

Regardless of your reporting line, should you not have regular private meetings with the senior independent director of your Board to discuss governance, accountability and ethical pressure?

Should you not commit to regular discussions with your team, and provide them with some training, on their professional and ethical responsibilities? Should there not be a clear and consistent understanding of how you, as General Counsel, interpret these principles?

Should you not report to the Chair of your Board any instances in which you feel anyone in your team has come under unacceptable ethical pressure?

Should you not seek to have an outside mentor who can both challenge and support you in what is often said to be a lonely, pressured role? At this time especially, is it not even more obviously essential to have a reliable sounding board for any concerns you may have?

What are your boundaries? What if you are bullied or your colleagues are bullied? What small misdemeanours by executive colleagues do you forgive? At what level of personal financial dependence on salary, bonus or shares are you starting to feel uncomfortable about your independence? How do you protect yourself and your team?

You can be on the team and still do these things. You are not being precious or other-worldly, you do not lack commerciality. You are not somehow locking yourself into an ivory tower if you care about what it means to be a lawyer. You are not diminished by wanting to uphold the highest possible standards of professional care and duty.

You can still be in the room.

I want you to be in the room. An amazing contributor, a wise and brilliant lawyer, a respected business colleague.

On this basis your team want you to be in the room.

On this basis the owners of your business should want you to be in the room.

Your profession wants you to be in the room.

Our Society needs you to be in the room.

July 2020

Tea drinking robots

...on a building site near you an animated discussion starts to get even more heated.

"I'm telling you every building site owner is going to replace their labourers with robot brick-layers"

"And I'm telling you, not here, not until the robots can scratch their arse and drink tea?"

"Man, listen to you, you just don't get it. They just lay bricks, you can even save the cost of tea."

"There is no just about bricklaying. That's your trouble. You got yourself a spreadsheet, a glass fronted fridge full of cool-aid, and a banker who can't remember your name but has asked you to mortgage your children, and suddenly you think you are James fucking Dyson. Bricklaying is not about laying bricks."

"Are you for real? I am telling you the robot bricklayers are more accurate, less wasteful and can work 24 hours a day without needing to scratch their arse or drink over-sugared tea. You cannot seriously turn this down"

"I am being deadly serious. You want to cut down a forest to plant a tree. You want to replace craft with function, pals with plastic and pride in achievement with a line of code. This really isn't just about laying bricks."

...At this point, I think we should leave them to it. I am sure there will be a mediation App with a $25 a subscription you cannot cancel popping up a screen near them any minute now.

Back in our worlds, as we emerge from the pandemic, like a storm that has passed through, there will be things lost we can never replace and memories that will be painful for years to come. We will need to adapt, and some things will never be quite the same again. However, in time there will be opportunity, and when there is, we need to be very clear how we ask our leaders to meet our needs. Our needs will be more than expediency, more than the lowest possible cost, and more than what "efficiency" alone can offer.

Leaders must show their people how they are proud of their individual contributions; to be valued for not just what they do, but how they do it as well. To be clear that everyone is more than a component of a vast cost versus income equation. At the same time, leadership is helping us see that we are all contributing to something more important than our individual pieces alone; to feel part of a team effort (even if we work remotely from each other) and that we are all connected to the end result. It is also helping us to be proud of who we work for, comfortable with how we trade and the impact we have on society and community.

If bricklaying was just about laying bricks, then bring on the robots. However, the wall is just one aspect of value. The person who builds the wall has pride in their skill, a sense of contribution to something more important, a memory of a difference made and of something that is a testimony to values which will live on long after they have left the site. That person is valued by their employer and colleagues, by their friends, family and community. That person has created something of value and something which will be valued perhaps for generations to come.

This level of contribution is not just a "soft" benefit. These things tie families and communities together and they create a foundation on which teams find they can do extraordinary things. We never just lay some bricks when we build a wall.

Does this mean we should never automate, or innovate or find a cheaper way? Of course not. It is part of life to see things evolve and improve and change. It is part of life to sometimes be disappointed and part of life to occasionally have to move on.

However if we could go back to the building site near you, and eves-drop on the conversation we left a moment ago, the issue was never about the greater efficiency of the robots. The issue was seeing that efficiency was only one aspect of value.

There are always multiple levels and types of value, and sometimes value is hidden from plain sight. Leadership is knowing the true value of something and the consequences of change. Leadership is to tread softly on our dreams.

Perhaps when we have taught our robots to drink tea, we can have more faith in the world they offer.

No need for daylight knobbery

How do you affect other people? What impact would you like to have?

What impact do others have on you? Is it the impact you would like them to have?

Is the affect you have on others the impact they would like you to have on them?

Some years ago, professional services businesses thought they had this stuff nailed. All hail the tech, training and process redesign that was CRM – Client Relationship Management. Management consultants and business gurus, like sweaty chimps in the banana aisle at ASDA, were falling over themselves to sell their own trade-marked "system", all beating their chests to the CRM beat.

And a little bit of me died inside.

If you fancy a cheese sandwich, the essential elements are the bread and the cheese plus your knowledge of where to locate these elements in your house. I put it to you, that you do not need a Cheese Relationship Management system. You do not need a process map, or to roll-out train-the-trainer academies, or an on-line multi-choice learning experience program. What you need is just to make a cheese sandwich.

I say professional services businesses do not need Client Relationship Management. We just need people to care about each other, and for business not to make us afraid to care.

Business has a habit of first making people fearful of making a mistake, then getting grumpy when people don't do things because of their fear of making a mistake. To overcome the fear that the business created, it will invest in expensive programs to train people to overcome the fear the business gave them. The training message is: "Don't be afraid to be yourself, unless being yourself is not good enough". However, this just creates a whole new level of fear. Business, then frustrated with the limited impact of the training, will ignore what it said the training was about, and promote the people who show no fear, while punishing the people who are still fearful.

Showing no fear in these circumstances is a lead indicator of daylight knobbery. It is the cleverest and surest way I know to ensure your arseholes rise to the top.

But surely, we need our people to have the right behaviours? The sort of behaviours that guarantee our success? Surely we need to tell them how to do this?

What I am about to say may sound harsh. I mean it to sound harsh. Professional services businesses for generations have secured the wealth of their owners by putting fees before behaviours. Expediency is the key value that unlocks success.

For too many businesses, leadership has become an oversimplified ambition to secure the wealth of the owners. The only judgement then applied to how this happens is based on one six-word question, "Does he bring the fees in?" The only time this gets even more chilling is when it becomes an eight-word question, "Yes but, does he bring the fees in?".

The world is changing, but we need to accelerate the pace of change. We do not need a process map to make a cheese sandwich and we do not need any Client Relationship Management systematic bollocks to be human.

The questions I posed at the start have their answers in the people we are.

How do you affect other people? Ask them. Listen to them.

What impact would you like to have? Be kind, and care, and see what happens.

What impact do others have on you? Tell them. Ask them to listen to you.

Is it the impact you would like them to have? Tell them. Ask them to keep listening to you.

Is the affect you have on others the impact they would like you to have on them? Ask them and keep listening to them.

You have wonderful gifts. A talent to learn, an intellect to admire, and skills that give you an opportunity to make the world a rather better place, one person at a time. Above all you are human. I think it might be a winning combination on planet Earth.

No need to be a trusted advisor, put the power pants down and listen.

I have long railed against the term "Trusted Advisor".

I think it verges on meaningless self-aggrandisement which flatters the title holder, but mystifies our colleagues who are not lawyers, while possibly diminishing the role of our other colleagues who are lawyers.

What is my status, I wonder, before I have climbed the giddy heights of being a (or is it "the") Trusted Advisor? I have never seen a role advertised where the need was for "a lawyer with potential to become trusted".

Other functions seem to survive without the epithet (no need for Trusted Finance, or Trusted HR), so I am a little perplexed that Trusted Advisor seems to matter to so many lawyers, even though it is a term used casually and defies precise definition. I decided therefore to reflect a little more on why the title seems to mean something and not just to rant about it, again.

My reflection is that the title is still misjudged and speaks more to the neediness of the role holder. However, I think I have understood better what it means and in this post I want to explore an alternative role to reframe "Trusted Advisor" so that it becomes more accessible, more inclusive and more relevant for today.

The self-importance of being earnest

Some lawyers are straining to make their advisory role sound more important. For some lawyers perhaps being just an advisor is not enough. Maybe it seems too passive, or too much of a secondary role. However, the focus on enhancing an advisory role with the prefix "trusted" feels flimsy.

In any corporate reality, no advisor role has the same power as that which is given to those who make the big decisions. Giving advice is also by its nature a rickety construct, often placed on uncertain and shifting foundations We all know the advice we can give is dependent on the quality of the information we can access, on how much time we have and, frankly, even our own mood. Our advice also requires a simplistic frame. A frame that tries to capture alternatives, but denies that everything is connected to everything.

On the one hand – this.On the other hand – something else.

On balance therefore – that.

Most of the words of advice we have ever given tend to do this; it is less a distillation of wisdom, and more an over-simplification of reality. This is not a criticism, and it can be helpful, but advice wants to simplify a reality to create a well-intentioned, but unnuanced choice.

For those lawyers who want to be seen as terribly commercial and decisive, or other strong-jawed, legs-apart adjectives, to be just an advisor may feel a little lightweight. The solution, it seems, is to pull on a pair of power pants and adopt the Trusted Advisor pose.

It is this emphasis that grates. The right instrument perhaps, but the wrong tune. Playing the wrong tune more loudly only serves to make it more jarring.

The importance of being in the room when it happens

I believe if we could step aside from our insecure ambition, there is a truly critical role to play. It is a role that puts us purposefully alongside our colleagues.

As already described, we should first park the word "Advisor" because I do not believe it is our advice that is needed most.

Our most important role is the space we create for decisions to be taken. A space for calm, for reflection and for decisions to be made well. This is especially so for our executive colleagues, but also for all colleagues making decisions. The gift they need most is the time to reflect, for their thoughts to be heard, and to be constructively challenged.

Our most precious role is when we seemingly slow down time and pause with people. We are the brake on the relentlessness of rushing deadlines, and we create moments for people to hear their own thoughts. It is this unconditional, non-judgemental, seemingly indulgent gift of a reflective pause in which thoughts are listened to that truly matters. Not our advice.

I believe this unlocks so much for us. When we listen brilliantly, people become more vulnerable because they are heard. When we pause with people these moments can be more important and more intimate than any other. These moments affirm, encourage and give confidence to what follows. It is a privilege to be in the room when it happens.

It is not our advice that matters. It is not important that we are a trusted advisor. It is far more that we are a trusted listener.

If we were to focus on our skills to help create pauses, to listen non-judgementally, but to challenge constructively, what a difference we would make.

Be the role, not the label

The trusted advisor label is everything that does not really matter. A self-appointed, self-regarding title that may sooth a more fragile ego. However, if our value is not the advice we give, but the pauses we create for others to decide, then we need to focus on the value we bring not the label.

Becoming a great listener is everything that matters in the world today. A crucial low ego role for someone who is generous with their time, kind, respectful. A creator of pauses and a curator of a calming, gentle and safe place for thoughts to rest and breathe.

If that sounds too wishy-washy for our strong jaw-line alpha brethren, this is precisely the role needed for good governance, for executive accountability, for independent challenge, for ethical leadership and for doing the right thing, always.

There is no need for power pants. The joy of this discovery for me is how it opens opportunity for all of us to develop our credentials in this space.

To put it a little crudely, you must have some balls to state you want to be a trusted advisor. It is all about you, and it excludes and diminishes others who are more self-aware. However, we can all care enough for a colleague (whether they are more senior than us, a peer or junior) to let their thoughts breathe. It is not about us, but about the person listened to, and the space we offer for them to be heard.

And the wonderful irony of all this, is that when we listen brilliantly, we are often asked what we think too. Then, when we speak in these moments of reflection and pause, our own words have more resonance and carry their message more deeply and more impactfully.

I hope this helps. I hope the ambition for all young lawyers may be to worry less about being a trusted advisor, and to relish more the privilege of becoming a great listener.

The triangle player and you

The triangle is the least consequential instrument in the school orchestra. The tool for the last one picked. A way to include everyone and to exclude no-one. It is a means to fulfil a benign and thoroughly unobjectionable ambition that everyone can play if they want to.

However, based on my school days, I have come to believe that it had a rather more insidious purpose. Aged nine, and loving music but without a hint of talent or of my potential, I was the triangle player and I ticked a box for the school.

I ticked the box that says everyone who wants to be in the orchestra can be in the orchestra. It was not however a benign tick. This tick allowed the teachers to focus only on kids already identified as talented, and simply to tolerate me in the least distracting way possible for them. It cut off my route to have any of their care and attention, and it excused them from all responsibility to nurture me.

Inevitably, when it was so boring and so unfulfilling, I asked to leave the orchestra. There was no soul-searching required from the school, they had fulfilled their brief. Instead a note was sent home about how disappointed the school was in me. I was never given an opportunity to play anything ever again.

The school had nothing to regret, nothing to feel guilty about. The school had been benign and inclusive. Unimpeachable. Unreproachable. I was the one to regret my decision and to feel guilt.

I see now that the school had created a system and a policy that effectively excluded me in plain sight, but it had done so in such a way that the school was absolved from any responsibility or guilt for excluding me. How unkind is that? I do not say it was the intention, but it was the effect, and unkindness is felt by the recipient just the same.

I wonder, who are the triangle players in your business?

Who are the people who hope for your care and attention to

thrive, but who leave, or fail slowly? Do they leave, or fail slowly, in part because of your benign inclusion policies and your well-intended diversity practices? Do those policies and practices serve mostly to absolve you from your guilt and not to truly make a difference for those who need you to care about them.

If you have a disappointingly wide gender pay divide, or if people of colour or from non-traditional backgrounds, are disproportionately under-represented in your senior roles, but at the same time you can stack your diversity and inclusion initiatives sky high, then two things are likely. Your policies and initiatives are working harder to make you feel better, than they are to fix the problem you say you want to fix.

I believe you when you say you want to change the world. I do not criticise your intention. However, if your policies have not changed the world, when are you going to change your policies?

The little boy, aged nine, was proud to be the triangle player at first. He wanted so much to be part of the orchestra, to fit in and to help make a wonderful sound. Instead he saw that he was never truly part of anything. The forced tolerance of his modest efforts hurt more than any outright rejection.

The invisible walls that perpetuate the status quo do more harm than any obvious barrier to change. Whether intended or not, the invisible walls serve to make the powerful feel good about themselves. They do not help the disadvantaged become powerful.

Worse than this, the invisible walls deny those who are disadvantaged the chance to even feel aggrieved. You are here, aren't you? You have the laws and policies you asked for, don't you? What more do you want?

How extraordinarily cruel is that?

May I therefore ask you to really care about the triangle players in your business, care about them like they play first violin.

Who tells your story

This post is inspired by a conversation I had on Friday with a lawyer who told me of such a gruelling story that I have hardly thought of anything else since. I will come to it shortly, but one of the reflections I have had about what I was told is of the nature and power of stories, and especially who tells the story.

History is all about who tells the story. There has to be a narrator because history is just too big otherwise. The whole of everything that has ever gone before. An almost infinite number of experiences, events, conversations, glances, tears, giggles, pain and fears. And all remembered differently by those who were there. Each memory an individual's version of the truth – what they saw from their vantage point, what they heard, what they felt. Each separate moment a multi-faceted experience. No one angle, or point in time, the same for any two people. Who tells the story is our entry point to understanding, but through their lens.

Then when we then reflect on past moments, we look at them through our own lens of our experiences and feelings as they are today. History fades or is enhanced or repainted with each new reflection of today's light upon it.

History therefore is not a singular, linear truth; it is a mine of buried memories which are extracted, refined and then traded. This is not to deny history or to disrespect its study, it is just to observe that the past was only real once, and for those who lived it.

It therefore feels imperative to be influential in our own stories. To do what we can while we can to make the difference. To be our narrator and not an extra in the scenes of our own lives.

The reflection for me is that I need to do more today. I need to speak up more because while I may not be powerful, I am not powerless. I need to trust my judgement more and not be overwhelmed by feeling small. History may make me pause, but it is not a weight to hold me down, it is instead the foundation on which to lay my contribution.

When I look back on my career, there was a reason I wanted to become a lawyer, but it was not to honour a profession steeped in traditions; I was in fact far more intimidated than I was inspired by its history. The reason I wanted to become a lawyer was to change things. This was not a grand ambition to alter the course of history. It was more to help make things a little fairer for people, one problem solved at a time.

The frame we are given as lawyers by our ethical code is an extraordinary gift that empowers influence. It requires that I must act in a way that upholds the constitutional principle of the rule of law, and the proper administration of justice. I must act in a way that upholds public trust and confidence in the solicitors' profession and in the legal services I provide. That I will act with independence, with honesty, with integrity, in a way that encourages equality, diversity and inclusion, and always in the best interests of each client.

This is not permission to sit back and marvel at our exceptionalism and privilege, instead it is a challenge to play our part. To make a difference. It saddens me hugely when senior lawyers downplay the importance of this frame. It is as if to discuss their ethical conduct is to question their innate goodness. I believe the frame is our shield and our weapon, we are lucky to have it and we should be proud to honour it.

As mentioned earlier, I spent some time this week listening to a lawyer pour out his heart to me on a call, as he described his loneliness when first fighting for what was right, but then resigning from a company in which he had discovered systemic fraud. I will be writing to him this weekend to offer all the support I can. He is a lawyer of exceptional courage. A hero. He played his part flawlessly, made his contribution and he was not found wanting, but he has lost his job and feels alone.

The company that employed him may write a different story and probably will. It will be a kind of history too, but not the truth. It is also possible that the lawyer's story may never be written. His story may not inform a wider world. His story may be lost in time, but it is the truth and it will live with me forever.

History is a big word that includes everything past. But not all history is told, and not all the history that is told is true. We know, however, that history informs and can inspire, let us therefore find the stories that speak to us and share them with others so that they can be inspired too. Most importantly of all, never forget your story. It is the one that counts most, and it should also be told.

Thoughtless

"What are you thinking?"

"Nothing."

"No, really, what are you thinking?"

"Really, nothing."

There are moments in the day when I have no purpose. I am inert. I think it might be when I am at my happiest. No pressure, no expectation, no objectives, no consequences. A perfect state of thinking about nothing.

I have wondered if it would be ok to have no purpose. My purpose is to have no purpose. A man who likes to sit with his thoughts, but not thinking about any of them.

Why do we have to be so driven? Why must there always be a goal or a bloody mission?

This a is a role description for a job I would apply for:

"Please be honest and kind. You know what we want and we trust you will help us succeed. Come into the office or stay home according to what is best for you and the work. Do what you can for others, but ask what you want for yourself as well. Work on what feels important, stop doing anything that is not important. Always say what you are doing and why. If people are rude, unkind or unfair, please say. Please never be rude or unkind or unfair yourself. Rest when you are tired, help others when they are tired. Take the holiday you need, but never judge anyone for taking more or less than you. Work is not more important that your physical health, well-being or family. We will be glad for what you can give us, and we will pay you fairly for it."

I suspect you may think this is Utopian bollocks, but let me share something of the role description that is more typically observable in real life:

"The work we ask you to do has little relation to the job description we gave you on hiring. Your annual objectives are disconnected from your day to day work. Most meetings you attend are poorly chaired, lack clarity and purpose and are nearly always sub-optimal. Around 80% of your work effort is delayed, postponed or cancelled. You are generally under-appreciated. You struggle to take all your holiday. Other people do not pull their weight and leave you exposed. There are people in your business who undermine you and others who creep you out. You think the CEO is a sociopath and the only way to get on is to be his cheerleader. You think the products and services are ok, but you are not that bothered about any of them. The weekend is your sanctuary."

If I may be indelicate, I think this is a worse kind of bollocks to my Utopian bollocks.

We accept dysfunction as an everyday reality, even though we are bright enough to know it is dysfunctional. Why? It can only be that we feel it is permanent and that we have to accept it, because surely no-one would sit down and invent this shit from scratch?!

I think it happens because when we join a company with optimism and hope, if we see some rubbish things, we do not want to call it out because we are brand new. We spend the first few months trying to make sense of it and why everyone seems to accept it. Then we question if it might be us and perhaps we are being unrealistic. At some point our priorities change from trying to understand if we are right about the dysfunction, to trying to fit in and not be too frustrated or undermined.

Those who thrive and rise to the top in dysfunctional workplaces have understood that the dysfunction works for them. The people they recruit must be like-minded enough to preserve their privileges. Those who are outliers have two options, find a way to cope or leave, but consequently NOTHING CHANGES.

When I sit without a thought in my head, I have disconnected myself from the madness. No purpose. No plastic values pinned to the walls. No "feedback is a gift", No stretch targets and no tolerating inadequate men using hierarchy to fan their egos.

As I emerge from my state of blissful thoughtlessness and reset to cope with what is real, I am cheered by the thought that kindness brings light into any environment. We are never completely in the dark if we are kind to someone or if they show kindness to us.

However sometimes kindness is not enough. Sometimes we must change things. The structures we think we cannot change are not built with concrete against our bare hands. They are held together by learned behaviours we have observed and followed over time.

We can change this with our self-awareness, our unthreatening enquiry, our offering of gentle alternatives, our believing in our judgement and trusting our feelings. It might not mean revolution, but it doesn't perpetuate the status quo either.

I would like to see a quiet and thoughtful momentum for something a little bit better, one step at a time.

I think it starts by sitting without thinking and allowing all the nonsense to take a walk without you.

The penny dropped

The penny dropped one day over a beer with my co-founder, Lawrence Smith.

For those of you who may not know him, Lawrence is the inspiration for 90% of what we do (I am being generous to myself there) and the only person I have ever worked with who has been right about everything. His greatest gift however is not being right, but in still making you feel that the ideas, approaches and conclusions you have drawn are just as valid and he has built on all your thoughtfulness to take your idea and tweaked it just a little.

Listening to Lawrence in conversation is to receive moments of wisdom casually dropped into your lap like a sanctuary seeking ladybird. Something beautifully formed, easy to know, hardly any weight at all, delightful to see and instantly appealing.

Over the beer Lawrence was talking to me about an especially tricky individual that was making our work a little uncomfortable. I started having a bit of moan about him and wondering why anyone so unsuited to a role had been given the job in the first place.

Then Lawrence said "No one ever applied for a job wanting to fail in it. No one ever wants to come to work to perform badly."

When this penny dropped, and I realised what he had just said, I knew I may have unfairly framed hundreds, may be thousands, of past conversations about performance and competency. It was salutary and I have never done it again since.

I think there are four significant factors that influence failure. Poor strategy, poor environment, poor implementation of strategy, and poor behaviour. In any team, in any workplace, an individual employee is, fairly, accountable for their behaviour, but it is the Executive leadership that is accountable for the other three factors.

If failing performance is a concern why is 100% of the remedial effort focussed on the individual? Is it any wonder that "performance management" feels unjust, overbearing and framed to be a negative experience? Is it any wonder that an individual might succumb over time to being surly, uncooperative and cynical?

It will be tempting at this point to remember the tiny handful of cases when an individual was a bad apple. I get that reaction and it is not unfair. However, there will be so many more people who have been unfairly maligned and labelled. Their only failure really was to stop pretending it was ok.

In kinder environments I hear management say "he's not a bad person, just a round peg in a square hole". This is only marginally better and it is still fundamentally lacking honesty. It would be improved considerably if management noted "He is a good person, but we have failed to find a way for him to shine."

I would like to leave you with this thought – next time you are told by a colleague about an especially difficult member of their team, someone who isn't competent or capable of performing at the level required, please do not jump on that employee too and assume the worst of them. Poor behaviour in the end is not to be tolerated and must be addressed. However, poor strategy, poor environments and more implementation of strategy should not to be tolerated either and should be addressed as well.

In the span of my career I think I have come across four or five toxic individuals and I am unrelenting in wanting to deal with them, not least for the terrible impact they have on others. However, the vast majority of people who have been labelled as uncooperating, change resistant, lacking energy, etc, etc, etc – have not failed, but have been failed by their leaders.

In a world that celebrates decisiveness, speed, and bold and ambitious machismo, hold a thought too for the weary, the long-serving, the reserved, the trapped and especially those who have a contrary view. Wisdom can be found in everyone, everywhere, not just in the alpha-lingua of market forces and in the expediency of the moment.

success-ish

There are some well-worn clichés about success and failure. "We learn most from our mistakes", is perhaps one of the best known, while Kipling's poem "If" is the totemic ballast for this exceedingly good line of enquiry. Then there are the acres of sporting analogies from "second is first loser" to Arsenal fans fondly intended encouragement to near neighbours Spurs, that despite their best endeavours in recent years "You've won fuck all" (although the foundation of confidence on which this observation is made, is more sandy that concretey).

I have had a thought for some time now that we need to reframe the emotional response to success and failure. Failure after all is, for most of us, our everyday lumpen porridge that keeps our feet on the ground; while success is mostly just the fickle rush of disturbed air as luck flies past our line of sight and ruffles our hair.

And yet the narrative of success and failure is designed to undermine us. Ninety-nine percent of the propaganda we receive is that failure, despite being what we know best, is a bad thing, that demeans and diminishes us as people. While success on the other hand, which is as common as hens' dentures couriered by flying pigs under a blue moon, is apparently and tantalisingly just one self-help book away.

For me, this compounds our sense of failing because if I cannot have a bikini ready tummy in three weeks while still eating chips and ale, I am more of a failure than I already think I am.

My lived experience is failure. It is wearing odd socks, or traffic lights that turn to red as I approach them, a missed call from someone I have been chasing up for weeks, or a forgotten birthday, or a missed work deadline, or being late for a meeting, or a parent's side-eye look about my life choices, or liking the wrong tweet... and so on, for ever.

Failure is normal, but we hope for more. When it comes to appraisal time, we have the long wait, twice postponed (at least) to find out if we have been graded "outstanding". While I understand that praise is nice, if it is from a tired bloke a grade above us who has cut-and-pasted something from last year, it really should not be something that matters.

Frankly, I long for the day when we will all cherish being "competent with development needs" and just relish the release of pressure that comes with a lower expectation.

It is just a bloody job after all. Who wants to be outstanding at work? I would prefer to be outstanding at watching cricket while holding a Melton Mowbray pork pie and a glass of something chilled and aspirationally unaffordable.

I suspect we make five hundred decisions a day and most of them work out sub-optimally. I suspect that every day we are the recipient of five-hundred more decisions, and most of these are not to our liking either. Proclaiming this as failure however is to put our lives into a forced ranking and deciding we are at risk of making ourselves redundant. We must stop. This is not failure; this is to breathe and to be alive.

Success is not just an imposter, like a plausible, subtly drawn secret agent living amongst us; success is like a caricature of a crashing foam-clad mascot at a ghastly children's party. A sugar-rush of mayhem.

I think of success as the person who sits too close to me in an empty carriage. We rarely tell that person to sit somewhere else, but we spend the rest of the journey wondering if we can move further away. Success is the overly loud person at the party, and where the kitchen is our sanctuary with the half-drunk glasses of cheap wine and the discarded cheesy snack wrappers and crumbs. Our safe space.

This is not me advocating for a lifetime of sub-optimal or denying the momentary fun of being centre of attention. It is just to note that our everyday challenge is not to climb mountains unassisted by oxygen or to discover a Nobel Prize in the attic; it is to find joy in the absurd, in the ordinary, in the routine and in the small moments of haplessness that afflict us all.

My stretch target for 2020 is to confront failure like a muddy-pawed puppy rather than a shit-flinging bear.

Onwards and sideways fellow travellers. This time-machine we call our lives is not to be driven like a bat out of hell to be gone when the morning alarm goes off. Instead we should sail gently with a sense of proportion, a connection with the people we love, and a destination that matters less. After all, two out of three ain't bad.

August 2020

In London. In Person

This week I had some meetings in London. A carriage to myself into Paddington, a station concourse with more staff than passengers, a tube journey where there were so many seats to choose from, I arrived at my destination before I could decide where to sit. My international hotel had twenty-five guests (I asked) and while the Covid trained reception team did their best to pass on corporate reassurances through their branded masks, their eyes, as eyes always do, gave a more reliable testimony of personal uncertainty and concern.

Meetings with clients took place in pleasant strolls along the Embankment or in Royal Parks. Gentle elbow bumps replaced the sometimes slightly awkward moment when one is not sure if it is one kiss or two, or a warm handshake and, or, a light hug. Conversation was easy and warm and kind. More personal than usual, dwelling on health, family and friends, and with none of the awkward Zoominess of the video conversation frame.

It felt so good to be with people again. It felt good to sense when a conversation should change course or to know that now was a good time to unwrap a small period of silence and to let it be. It felt good to be preoccupied with someone else's story, and not to be preoccupied by the light in your room, or the arrangement of books behind you.

However, there was also melancholy in the air. Walking back to my near empty hotel, the streets were not thronged, and the cafes and bars were mostly closed. This silence, for London, was uncomfortable to hear. A quiet city is at first stunningly beautiful, but soon becomes a challenge to one's senses. A million stories not being told, lives and plans and hopes on hold. The silence a makeshift stage for our fears to play to their socially distanced audience of one.

As I walked, I wondered if business would ever be the same again; but as my meetings from earlier in the day had shown me, business is not a building. Commerce is not a contract. Strategy is not anything at all. Everything is people. Gigabytes of syllables, a billion emotions an hour running along superhighways of love, kindness, hopes and fears. Proximity is not a distance, but a feeling created by people who do not need a password to connect.

We need to get back to work, but not for the work. We need to congregate at events again, but not for the music or the sport. We need to see things together again, but not for the things we look at together. These things simply provide the cover stories for us to be human.

An experience which is not shared is a cardboard cut-out version of the real thing. It is the sharing of the experience that gives it depth and shape and substance, and life.

People often ask me, "how is your business Paul?" and I waffle on about this and that, and try not to overshare or underplay. However, after my two days in London this week, the question is much easier to answer. There is no business.

There is nothing to touch, or pick up or to take a selfie with; there is nothing that exists separately that has an opinion or a life of its own. There is just us and the time we spend with each other, thinking about each other, helping each other and the shared experience which then becomes a shared memory.

Covid is teaching me that we had over-relied on an office address, with its policies, processes and hierarchies, to make our working lives seem meaningful. I suspect the truth is that these things provided a mostly inconsequential backdrop to what is truly important – and that is how we make each other feel.

The lesson I am reflecting upon, after my two days in London this week is that being truly present with people energises creativity, sparks thoughtfulness, dampens anxiety, lessens selfishness, challenges our thinking, unsettles our lazy notions, reaffirms an affection to learn and grow, and above all honours our opportunity to make a positive difference to other people in this world.

It's ok not to put your hand up

"And the gym opens at 6am"

I think this might be the most redundant line ever uttered to me in the whole span of my life.

It's funny what we reflect upon sometimes; how thoughts from nowhere pop into our minds, linger for a moment, and then they're gone, perhaps forever.

Spending two days in London a week or so back, I stayed in an unfamiliar hotel, but the receptionist's charming monologue had a familiar sound...

"Breakfast is served from 7am, and the gym opens..." she paused, caught her thoughts and then continued "...I'm afraid the gym is still closed."

I smiled at her pause and reassured her that I was glad to be here, the lack of a gym would not be a disappointment to me. In doing so, I spared her my own well-rehearsed and terribly amusing lines that men of a certain age should neither exert themselves in shorts, nor drip their perspiration closer than one half-mile from another human being.

As I took my room key from her and found the lift to my room, I had a little thought about how many of my lines are so well trodden that their meaning is no longer visible to me. I trot them out like a tired comic's old gags, but while they may sometimes raise a half-smile somewhere in the room, I wondered if they are relevant today, useful today or even wanted today?

At what point in our lives do we move from being people who predominantly listen, to people who predominantly broadcast?

I once used to sit on a worthy committee where one fellow member would regularly haul himself from his seat like a great sail being pulled up a mast, then clasping his thumbs to his lapels he would lean back, take an implausibly long breath, pause again and then drench us with his opinions – "My views on this subject are well known, but I suggest they stand repeating..."

I am not sure if you have seen a collective eye-roll before, but it is quite something to see a room full of bright, articulate and often sassy individuals paralysed by politeness, so that the only act of rebellion left open to them is to be determined not to listen.

I sometimes draw on things I remember from my childhood and as a quiet, rather nervous schoolboy I would rarely (never) be the person who thrust their hand skyward pleading for the teacher to pick them out. Even today, if I am in an audience and the presenter asks for a show of hands on something, I am ridiculously gripped by a slight panic not to put my hand up.

After one lesson the teacher asked me to stay behind for a minute. With the classroom empty, he asked me very gently why I never put my hand up. I said something to the effect that I didn't think I had anything to say that would not be said by someone else, and said better than I would say it.

I don't remember exactly what he said to me, but it was something like this:

"That's fine, as long as you know that clever people are not always right, and those who do not think themselves clever will often be wise. Always listen Paul, always hear what has been said. Understanding is what happens after we have listened, not before it has been said"

He told me that it was ok not to put my hand up, as long as I was listening.

On that day one of my fears got left behind. I knew I had found a way to accept there was more for me to learn from listening than from being preoccupied with why I was not talking.

As I put my bag down on my bed in my unfamiliar hotel with the gym that would not be open at 6am, I was pleased that I had listened to the young receptionist and noted the pause in her unfamiliar lines. I was even more pleased I had not swamped such a delicate moment of understanding with my own lump of a well-worn broadcast-ready reply.

You've messed it up and you know you have

I may be a little tired and ragged. Perhaps the heat has sapped my patience too, but I need to rant. I think for the first time in my life I am witnessing a Government's inner circle prepared to indulge in wilful incompetence.

A-Level results moderated by algorithm is the latest example and a metaphor for our times.

A small group of politicians who distrust experts so much (in this case teachers) that they have sanctioned a technology that is palpably unjust, and yet they still hold to its incredulous results. All to serve their insatiable belief in their own infallible self-regard. The magic thinking is that their algorithm must be a better test than the lived experience of teachers and students who actually did the work, together, in a classroom over the last two years.

Similarly, we have had a failed "Track and Trace" app for Covid that was meant to be "world beating", and non-existent border technology for Brexit that was meant to enable frictionless trade. Instead we could not track or trace a Minister with a clue, and we risk turning Kent into a lorry park of such a scale that the International Space Station will have a new landmark to navigate by.

Real experts with real expertise are disparaged for, presumably, failing to be a disciple of those with magic thinking. The sort of magic thinking that flows from a mandate from "the People" to promise what cannot be delivered. However, magic thinking also ensures that there is no such thing as failure, just an opportunity to spend fortunes (of our money) to fund outrageously speculative solutions.

This is the logic of the addicted gambler playing longer and longer odds to recoup what is already lost. He sells everything including his soul, but with a con-man's smile and a hint of what the hell have I got to lose.

Meanwhile people have died who should be alive; businesses have failed that could still be trading and now students will carry a lifetime of "what if" anxiety – and for what? Mostly, it seems to me, to keep a few super-inflated egos topped-up with the noxious gas of populism and a rubber tube fitted to whiff their own shameless arrogance.

Leadership in public life used to mean something important, now the playbook says never apologise, double-down; insult rather than debate, assert rather than test, bully don't listen, sack dissenters and then personalise the criticism of them. Drive on, no map required, because the mandate we have is to do whatever we like.

In the end we are all gas-lit to the point of wondering if we might be making too much of it all. After all, at least this isn't America, and there is football back on the telly, and we can go to the pub. But we're not making too much of it all. This is lazy, careless, destructive, shameless, self-aggrandising and self-amused naughty boy politics.

It has long been said that power corrupts, but I think it is worse than that this time. Corruption is a contained irritant. It is something that leaves a stain, but one that can be cleaned up. What we are seeing now is that power corrodes. It is disfiguring public life in general, and scarring generations for possibly decades to come.

This is not something to make fun of in a satirical half hour on TV, this is the debasement of our values, our communities, our hopes. It is a disgrace.

Mistakes are forgivable. Making the wrong call when not all the information is available is not shameful, and caring counts for a lot. However, this is not what is happening. Time, after time, after time we are being played.

Public health matters less than backing your mates. Pretending you protected care homes matters more than the lessons you could learn from a catastrophic mis-judgment. Throwing money at implausible technology is better than admitting we might have got things wrong. Buying ferries that do not exit and PPE that does not protect is just so much whiff-whaff. What's a few million quid among donors and loyal friends? As for close family, obviously, let's give a peerage to our little brother because we had to be a bit beastly to him over supper last year.

Now, the primus knobhead inter pares is pouring anxiety over thousands of teenagers for no better reason than to do the right thing would reveal an uncomfortable truth about the whole sorry shitshow he leads. It is all utterly, utterly damning. You cannot op-ed your way out of this. Simply put, lives have been wrecked for your sense of infallible entitlement.

Born to lead? Chosen to succeed? My arse.

Take care everyone, I'm sorry for ranting. Rant over.

The extraordinary smallness of you

Talk of a Covid silver-lining risks being completely insensitive to the hardships, and grieving, that many individuals, families and communities have suffered and continue to suffer. I do not want to write something therefore that sounds like a half-hearted call to whistle "Always look on the bri-i-ight side of life…"

It is because of the hardship and grief, not in spite of it, we should reflect on whether we should rush to re-create what we had before if it did not serve us so well. Reflection, however, is one of those words that now carries a degree of privilege. Many people will simply think – "It's all very well saying we should reflect, but some of us are too busy just trying to get through each day". I think this is a fair enough challenge. Reflection is a privilege, but then even more reason to do it, if lucky enough to have that luxury. I would like to share a reflection with you.

To begin with, I'm not sure we need to reflect on things like the pros and cons of working from home, or about different video technology platforms or even what value looks like, because in a way we have already moved way beyond what we thought was settled thinking. It seems clear right now that business travel will never go back to the way it was before. It is clear we will do more work and be more productive away from traditional offices environments; and it is also clear that our leaders will have no choice but to trust that their colleagues will do what has to be done. This is how it is now, and we will not go back.

Of course, businesses will want to grow, and colleagues will want to thrive and be successful. Their job titles and the number of direct reports they have will still count for something, but something is different. We are less puffed up. We have become human-sized again. Reduced to normal.

We are no longer defined by the floor we work on, the places we lunch, whether we turn left or right on planes or if we are too busy for small talk. We are all, fundamentally, just ourselves, exposed and vulnerable. We are more reliant on noticing others and being noticed by others to get things done.

At first, I wondered if people who were very confident and self-reliant would do better; but this is like having a fridge full of food. Great for a while, but sooner or later we need to replenish. The workplace is the same, we need to be replenished too. What I have seen is that the need to be replenished is much less about career advancement, a bonus or a job title; and much more about others noticing that we have a hinterland that we care deeply about. Our children, our parents, our friends, our pets and the opportunity to meet in person.

We have pulled away from the corporate imagery, and relied less on the projected hologram of our office persona. We have shrunk our egos and lessened the noise around us; we have become more real.

And now I think something extraordinary has happened. We can see everyone. We can hear everyone. We notice what is said and we can notice if what we say is being heard.

No longer, a place that is just for a few, an arena show where the players are projected on to giant screens. We are all now playing an acoustic set. A place where we care about the harmonies and where a missed note is heard, and not drowned out by the relentless amplification of those who hold the mic.

As summer folds itself away and thoughts turn to unpacking what will be next, I hope we will remember the precious smallness of our humanity and value it more than the artificial grandness of what we seemed to care about before.

When we are back in meeting rooms again, we will be changed.

We will not be able to pretend that we do not know our stories. We will listen more to the quiet voices. We will share more because we know how isolating it is not to be left in the dark. We will not judge people by the time they arrive or leave, but for the difference they make. We will appreciate being noticed, and we will notice others more, because to notice is to care.

None of this is the enemy of efficiency or competency. None of this costs the bottom line dear. And none of it is a Pollyanna pipe-dream.

We have all seen, heard and felt what it is like to be vulnerable, and we have all seen and heard others be vulnerable with us.

We are richer as a result. We are all less hidden, more equal, heard more, noticed more and, as a result, we can all be valued more.

Leading together

Why do so many leaders allude to feelings of loneliness in their roles?

Is there an expectation that stepping into such roles there will be times when the weight of responsibility, and its accompanying accountability, will feel like a solitary endeavour?

I would like to share a thought. I don't say it applies to everyone, but I know it applies to some.

Leadership comes with a large laundry bag of well-worn myths and clichés. We all have examples of those we have seen do well (and less well) with its responsibility; and we may ourselves know the feeling of what it is like when we had that responsibility too. But why would it feel lonely? Loneliness is a very specific and emotive descriptor that conjures a sense of isolation, of lacking support, of being friendless. It feels deeply uncomfortable.

Before I go further, I know very well that we can feel lonely in a crowded room, that we can feel unsupported despite offers of help and that we can be cautious about who we allow to be close to our heart. I am not dismissive of the emotional weight of responsibility and how this might, for some of us, feel that it takes the air from our lungs and glues us to behaviours we cannot seem to move away from. However, I also want to suggest that some of us may, some of the time, have been the author of our own sense of solitude. Sometimes we are the architect of our emotional exile.

Remember when we were young? The feedback we often cherished was positive, ambitious and affirming, but such feedback might also sew the seeds of our later fully grown vulnerability. I imagine something like this might have been be said:

"Paul gets things done. He is a self-starter, decisive, has good judgement and copes well under pressure. A future leader for sure".

We would all be flattered, wouldn't we? I think we would all bank that description and let it become a corporate truth about our credentials. Then, following our promotion a year or so later, the Chief Executive might send a warm message around the whole office:

"I am delighted to welcome Paul to the executive team. A good mind, a track record of delivering and someone we all can rely on to get things done."

Again, we would share this our mum and have a quiet "look at me" moment. All upside, right?

However, these patterns of feedback are reinforcing behavioural expectations; in truth they are laying down tramlines to a destination that is a hollowed-out version of our hopes and expectations. If we are not careful our route is now fixed, and it is a pathway to nowhere we should want to go, because how do you ask for help when you are the guy who always gets things done? How do you admit to feeling inadequate when the corporate truth says that we are all reliant on you? How do you tell us that you need support, when your role is to support us?

I say this cautiously, and I know it is not for everyone, but we should not let leadership myths and flattery be the threads from which we try to weave our own leadership style. It is not good for us; it is not good for those we want to help and most importantly of all it is not good for those who want to help us.

Leadership is about character. It is about people who care, who want to effect change and make a difference. Leadership therefore is about all of us, and for all of us, because in this way we are all leaders.

In this way we are also all vulnerable. We do not know everything. We do not have limitless energy. We are often wrong and we will cry when we are overwhelmed. These things are also leadership behaviours.

My hope is that the warm note from the Chief Executive I mentioned earlier, might in future say something like this:

"I am delighted to welcome Paul to the executive team. A good mind, a track record of delivering and someone we all can rely on to get things done. He is also terrible at asking for help, so help him anyway. He will get things wrong too, so he'll need you to point things out. And while he is a good person, he is definitely not a superhero, so look after him please."

Leadership is not a fantasy story of heroic daring do, it is a complex undulating narrative of how we learn to help people be their best, and how we learn to allow those same people to help us be our best too.

It should not be lonely. We should try not to follow a path where we find ourselves alone. Leadership is a shared endeavour, one where we are vulnerable together, but where we can also shine together. Please take care.

September 2020

The play within the play

Is a play really a play if it does not have an audience?

Is not our part (perhaps described as row N seat 23, the quiet fidget, absorbed, stifling a cough, holding a sweet wrapper in the dark) part of the play too? Even though we are not seen until the very end when the lights go up, do we not bring the validation, the energy and the reason for it to be?

When tomorrow comes, I wonder will it arrive with that feeling of air being pulled from our lungs with the clattering whoosh of the fast train hurtling through the station; or will it loll semi-consciously out of its crumpled bed like an old dog uncertain of where to put its feet?

When tomorrow leaves us will it do so with a gentle sigh, and a tummy full feeling before snuggling into sweet dreams? or will it wrestle us into a half sleep with indigestible worries and jagged lists of things not done?

Will our next working day be a patchwork quilt of hope, indifference, joy, frustration, surprise, boredom and success? Or a tangled heap of miscellaneous random wires belonging to things we cannot find, do not recall having, or ever remember needing?

Is our next business meeting, a microcosm of all we dislike about small-minded point-scoring and predictable what's-the-point-anyway cynicism; or will it be a chance to be the energy for someone else, to respect another point of view and to feel acknowledged?

Some of these feelings, and all shades of them, will be our feelings each and every day; and it is because we have these feelings that we are also players. We are never not involved. Even when we sit in the gods, far from the stage, we play our part. We are always in the story.

While all the world is a stage, we are the play within the play, within the play.

I am not saying this with the expectation that we will now run from the stalls, seize the spotlight and close the show with our mesmerising oratory. I know for sure that this is not my part and I do not want it to be my part. I say it however for all of us who need the scene to be small enough for us to be at home in it and to make the difference that we can make.

There is always a play within the play, within the play where we are the actors with the lines that count; where we can be kind, where we can listen and be the difference. There is always a scene where we can be the reason someone else shines and for us to shine too.

No matter how big or small our part may seem, we are in the play and our part is always important.

It was twenty years ago today...

It was twenty years ago today, on 12 September 2000, that a thirty-eight-year-old lawyer and recently former General Counsel of two different financial institutions bubble-wrapped his career and left it behind in a sort of Big Yellow jobs storage facility. It was time to hitch a trailer of his half-formed thoughts and to wobble unsteadily into the future steering away from the well-worn career path.

LBC Wise Counsel is twenty years old.

I am sometimes asked why I gave up being a General Counsel as if I must have been very brave or very mad. The truth about the decision in 2000 however was that I didn't think I was giving up being a General Counsel; I was just not doing it for a while. If the intrepid wanderer with his half-formed thoughts ran out of puff, my expectation was that I would simply go back, obviously. The moment of realisation that this would never happen was some years later when I reflected quietly that I might have wandered far too deep into the unconventional forest to find my way back out again.

Anyway, I do not want to make this a self-indulgent piece about me, and I am not going to reminisce about all the bars, burgers and airports. Twenty years however is a long time and I would like to share a few reflections. In doing so I should also say that I am not claiming special insights or truths that you must accept and carry forward; we should always carry the experiences of others as lightly as we can, so there is room for our own. For what it is worth, in twenty years of supporting, working alongside and mentoring lawyers, here are a few thoughts I believe to be true...

Your clever idea may be innovative, ground-breaking and brilliant, but it matters very little unless you also know how to make change happen. Change does not happen because you have announced it. Change happens because you can persuade people to come with you.

You can only persuade people to come with you if they trust you. People will only trust you if you have cared enough to listen and respect what you have heard.

The industrialisation and commoditisation of leadership has meant that we have outsourced our humanity to data. We need to reclaim it. Good data helps leadership, but should not define it. Leaders have to shine in three human ways – to ask for help with humility and good grace; to know their people and to care for their well-being and success; and to be consistent, clear and credible in their relationships, communication and ambitions.

Small acts of thoughtful care matter hugely. On the other hand, most transformational change projects are rank, risible bollocks. They are the vain-glorious distractions of short-term, ego driven, fantasy management. Their fundamental flaw is how they neglect small acts of thoughtful care. Culture is created on such small acts which are always seen and felt, but are never written down. Culture is not an initiative or a manual and it is definitely not about empty rhetoric. People are indeed your greatest asset, but it is a meaningless slogan if you do not know someone's name and their story.

Leaders should be accountable but not lonely. We should all listen more, talk a little less, be generous with our time, say how we feel and never sacrifice our health for work. There are also wonderful cultural differences that we can observe, learn from and respect in our dealings around the world. However, I have never worked with anyone who did not appreciate and respond to humility, kindness and promises kept.

I now firmly believe that career paths do not really matter, but what does matter is finding a place to work where you are listened to, can grow and make a difference. Your best role is one where you can thrive. Search for places where you can thrive, not for places that pay you more or flatter your sense of what you deserve.

In this regard please value time above wealth or status. Time is a gift, but it is also the ultimate use-once only product with guaranteed built-in obsolescence. A role that gives you time to think, time to grow, time to help others, and time for your family and friends is a role you can love and hold dear. But when it is not like this be careful. When time is stolen from you, the erosion of our confidence and well-being that results burns deeply on our souls. Long grinding hours, coercive low-level bullying, injustice, discrimination, unkindness, fear and anxiety stay with us forever. Be careful. Be kind to yourself.

Finally, the role of lawyers has never been more important, never been more needed, never been more vulnerable. From the criminal justice system, to the rule of law, to the climate crisis, to our moral compass in business and in our communities. It is not our time to be a spectator. I urge you please to have a view, and to know your own "red lines". Courage is not always a David and Goliath act of epic heroism, but it is still courageous to stand firm about doing the right thing in what to others might seem a non-descript meeting where no-one else cares. We need to be courageous every day, but please relish your role because there has never been a more important time for us to be at our best.

LBC Wise Counsel's twentieth anniversary should have been a time we could share our appreciation with you in person with and to thank so many people. The kindness, generosity and love we have received has been our inspiration and our motivation. We are truly blessed and truly grateful. The thirty-eight-year-old former GC would not have believed how lucky he could possibly be, even if he still has the look of someone wandering lost in a forest.

What will we take with us?

An odd question I heard someone ask this week was "if your house was on fire, and all people and pets were safe, what one possession would you hope could be rescued?"

In the context in which the question was asked, we had only a moment to think of an answer. The answers varied from treasured framed photographs, to items of sentimental rather than monetary value, to an item of clothing belonging to a dear parent who had recently died.

It was just a game, but it still reveals something of what we actually value, rather than what is valuable from an insurance claim point of view. As the conversations moved on, however and the game was forgotten by most of us, I was stuck with my thoughts. I wondered to myself, if it was not my house, but my career that was on fire, what one thing would I like to rescue?

Careers, of course, are never literally on fire, but what if your role is unexpectedly redundant? What if that "nailed on" promotion goes to someone else? What if your business collapses and everyone in it is out of work in a moment?

In these circumstances what is the metaphorical possession you clasp dearly to your chest, as you walk from the smoking embers of the job you thought was secure?

Is it your Russell Group 2:1, or the big city law firm training contract, or your biggest deal, or your airport lounge gold pass, or your job title? I wonder if these things truly define our need to feel fulfilled in a career, or whether these Things are like the replaceable ornaments that decorate a room, but which in the end do not define us.

Very sadly, I fear that many of us will experience a sudden loss of something important in the next twelve months. It is impossible to imagine that every role will be preserved, and that the economy will be buoyant enough for every business to survive. Change will certainly come and with it, for some, that sudden upheaval and sense of loss, anger, frustration and, indeed, a sort of grief.

I do not anticipate it as a certainty, but I do feel we should reflect on how we will cope.

What do you value about your career at this point that you must take with you if your current role were suddenly to end? When you have to scramble, a little dazed, from what seemed certain, to a place of great uncertainty, what are you holding against your heart?

If I reflect on my own world, which is (as it always has been) fragile and uncertain, then some things are hugely sustaining to me. For example, I know that the tasks, the meetings, the reports etc, matter very little indeed. What matters most are the relationships we have with clients, and faculty and suppliers. Relationships that will prevail and become even more valuable in times of great need.

I know as well that the greatest achievement is never revealed in a balance sheet or in a set of management accounts; the greatest achievement is in the difference we make to those who put their trust in our work. Nothing can take that away.

Kindness too is an investment that creates an invisible network of support. The more we offer, the more secure the network becomes. Each strand of kindness is the perfect gift that costs nothing but thoughtfulness, and yet can never be wasted. Kindness stays with us, and softens the jagged edges of life. Its miracle is how we never really know how it works, just that it always will. The smallest and the seemingly least consequential moment can literally change a life. I remember well (and will never forget) the letter a college lecturer wrote to the senior partner of the law firm I hoped to join, recommending me to the firm. The letter might have taken ten minutes to write, but it undoubtedly changed my life.

If the fire alarm goes off on your current role and you must evacuate this moment of your career, I hope you can take with you the care of relationships that matter and the difference you made to others. At a time when you might feel scared and overwhelmed, these things will matter more than anything. These things speak for you when you might be lost for words.

I never want anyone to experience that sudden loss, but it has always happened in the past to some, and it will happen again to others.

The care we take now, and every day, to look after the things we should take with us, will bring fulfilment today and sustain us later. When we walk from the building for the last time, I hope we can walk in the certain knowledge that we made a difference. It is that investment that will never let us down.

Our gifts are real, don't fade away

As a teenager I might not have been the edgiest individual you could meet.

My record collection included ELO and the Carpenters. In the 5th form I went to a house party, once, but I didn't like the noise, or cider, and I seemed to be the only person washing-up used glasses. When other boys started to ride obscure Czech made 50cc motorbikes, I preferred a quiet evening in listening to football commentary with expert summarising by the ever sensible Trevor Brooking.

I have always been quiet. Kind people might say I am shy and thoughtful, others might miss I was even there.

Fast-forward forty-three years and the same fifteen-year-old boy still lives within me. Mr Blue Sky makes me smile, I really do not like cider and I will not leave dirty glasses in the sink overnight. I am always quiet with strangers and would much prefer to go unnoticed.

These things have not changed. They make me, me.

However, if you had said to me as a lad that one day I would be a lawyer, an executive, a presenter, a writer and a mentor, literally none of it would have been believable. I had no idea that quiet, shy, insecure people could have varied and wonderful careers like confident, gregarious and assuredly talented people do.

I do not believe I am special, and so this is not the time when I reveal my inner West Coast, head-mic wearing, leadership evangelist. I do not believe if you want something badly enough then you can achieve anything you want. That exhortation mostly oils the egos of those who can thread bollocks on a string of cliches. It also burdens anyone who has not achieved what they want with not wanting it enough. That's unkind, arrogantly judgemental and wrong. Therefore, if like me, you already feel a level of insecurity about what you offer the world, may I suggest that a loudly confident, Botox-riddled millionaire on a You Tube subscription, is a sub-optimal cul-de-sac for our needs.

I do believe, however, that we all have gifts which offer a lifetime's permission for exploration and growth. I believe the gifts we have at our fingertips, are all the gifts we need to find our way. It turns out, for example, that the quiet lad who doesn't like noisy parties is quite good at creating a thoughtful space where others feel comfortable to share their stories.

It is why I am not a fan of artificial appraisal processes, whether forced ranking, or so called balanced scorecards, or all the other faddy over-simplified development models. They all tend to herd us into hypothetical two-dimensional pens where we can all bleat in unison. We become a statistical distribution rather than a community of talents, opportunities and interests. Over time we lose sight of our potential and settle for an alignment to sterile competencies.

A career is not a thirty year trolly dash to collect titles, equity, and bonuses, nor is it a free-style rock climb to the summit of the latest org chart. A career is our nuanced, complex and (I hope) fulfilling exploration of understanding what we offer the world and finding those places where that offer is needed most and where we can thrive.

We are conditioned to believe that careers should have a linear progression. We often interpret events as if we are in a race or competition, and as a result we are all at risk of failure in a game that serves little purpose save that it exalts a few, but undermines the majority, and in doing so often cheapens the many gifts we bring.

In the end, such a frame for our careers denies the world the opportunity to benefit from our potential. But what if careers had a different frame? One that was not defined by systems, "models", data analytics, or by the embedded conscious and unconscious biases of several generations of, mainly, alpha-male bosses. What if we made our own frame for our career so that it is not an ill-fitting hand-me-down that hides our needs in a cloak of indifference? What if, instead, it could be a lifelong, complex, colourful patchwork where family pieces are stitched to every funny, misshapen, sad, hectic or reflective experience; a frame where we also understand and relish the joy of exploring where our gifts might take us.

I know of course that mortgages must be paid, that responsibilities are paramount and that compromises and sacrifices are woven into the fabric of each and every day. I am not advocating selfishness or a cavalier disregard for the economic needs of the moment. What I do ask, however, is that from time to time we pause to appreciate and understand the wonderful gifts that we have at our fingertips. I want us to know them and to love them. I want us to feel our potential and to know we can explore it in different ways, at different times. I want us to feel that there are always people who have stories like ours who can inspire and mentor our journey; and I want us to know that if we feel a little bit left behind, we are not defined by our current role, salary or the capriciousness of any negative moment in time.

Our responsibility is to love the gifts we have. We are here to make our difference in our way, in our time. It is our career and they are our gifts. We loan these things to others while we work with them for now, but they are ours to take elsewhere if we find our gifts are not valued enough. We should not let our gifts, or our potential, fade away.

October 2020

When the meeting ends

There is a very special place that we have all known so well, but rarely visit any more.

A place we may not have valued quite as much as we should have valued it before.

A place we may be missing without even realising it has gone, or that it was a place at all.

It is a place where our guard is a little lower, and where we see people in a little more colour.

It is a liminal space that has a cast of players all following their own unscripted roles. It is the scene we play when a meeting ends; the performance of how we leave the meeting room.

There are the lingerers and the note-takers. There are the reflective-pausers, the dasher-offers, the tidier-uppers, and the straight-back-to-their-phoners checking what they have missed.

This play unfolds over a couple of minutes. It always ends with an empty room, but what takes place between the end of the meeting and the empty room helps to set our mood for what is to come. It can energise, deflate, frustrate, sadden or inspire, but it is always an important moment of unscripted disconnecting. We know how we feel, and we can sense how others may feel too. We have a map of emotional contours to help guide us through what comes next.

Now it is gone. Instead we meet from our Zoom laden aeries, and we disconnect from meetings in a completely different way.

We are shut out and shut down in an instant from the virtual reality. There is no going back to pick up a forgotten pen, no quick words in a doorway, no knowing looks. No liminal pause. No time for care, clarification, reassurance and encouragement, or for our "I'm absolutely fine" smile to be understood to mean "You know I'm not really fine at all".

Meetings have lost a bit of soul and no amount of digital jazz-hands as the meeting link casts us out, feels like an adequate replacement for the sound of chairs being pushed back and the moments of human improv that always follow.

It has made me wonder what other liminal pauses we have lost.

Those moments of unplanned casual connection that link the planned and anticipated structure of our working day. Liminal pauses like the silent lift shuffle; or the morning arrival conversation, or are-you-doing-anything-nice-this-evening conversation. Or the do-you-have-a-minute conversation and the fancy-seeing-you-here conversation. Or the nearly always unnerving, chief executive-catches-your-eye-and-remembers-she-asked-you-to-do-something-for-her conversation.

The liminal pause will never be an objective, or a target or a metric or a process. The liminal pause will not be the first thing you think of as crucial to your day. Liminal pauses however are the breaths we take to oxygenate our working life. They are casual but crucial to our understanding of how we think about our work, our colleagues, our sense of place, our worth and our need to belong.

Remote working has largely stripped them from our day. We now live in mocked-up miniature television studios of flattened reality. Some of us are happy to allow the world behind us to be glimpsed. Others have framed a view that offers no clues. Some of us have chosen a virtual background or for the camera to be turned off. We are hidden in plain sight.

Whatever happened to the lingerers, the reflective pausers and all our other liminal heroes. No more liminal anymore.

The side-bar chat function, the separate subversive Snapchat group, or the swapping of emojis, are the nearest things we have found; but they are still only a synthetic pause. Meta maybe, not liminal.

To be honest I am not sure we have realised how important these pauses are for us. I think we need to find the times and the places for liminal pauses with each other again. The place to improv without agendas, papers, or actions; a place that is not defined, but just to be.

The next time someone asks you if you need something, ask them to be with you for a liminal pause.

Even just to talk about one may turn out to be one.

The discomfort zone

If the weakness in your argument is the place you linger when others have moved on...

If the shortcomings you perceive in your experience cast a shadow over your confidence to do the role you have wanted for a while...

If the negative feedback you received years ago still kicks your shins; and if your development needs today are the wailing illegitimate children such feedback drags behind its half-baked truths...

Then welcome, my friend, to the discomfort zone.

For all the mentoring hours, now over 20 years, it has been my privilege to share with people of all backgrounds and experience it is an incontrovertible truth that they are rarely undone by their lack of expertise, or the weight of responsibility, or for lacking a desire to achieve. They will, however, often describe their contribution in ways that supress their quiet and unassuming potential, and instead amplify their unruly, discordant self-critic. When we need to believe in ourselves, we can sometimes be a poor friend to our vulnerabilities.

On the spectrum of self-love, we can all find a gentler, kinder place to rest. There is plenty of room without having to be near the over-reaching preening knob end; or to be at the standing-alone-in-the-rain-when-the-last-bus-has-gone end.

The phrase "imposter syndrome" is used widely and I think we all have a sense of our own relationship with it. However, I am not writing this to be a rousing piece about how to overcome our imposter syndrome. Indeed I am not even sure it is something to overcome. Nor do I think we should pretend it is doesn't matter by holding hands swaying to Kumbaya. This will not sustain us when we are alone again, facing our fears again.

I would like to offer a different view; a view that says the reason we might be uncomfortable is because things are uncomfortable. The reason we might feel at the edge of our experience is because we have not done this before. The reason we are feeling stressed is because what we are doing is stressful.

Perhaps our imposter syndrome is with us not to undermine us, but to protect us. It is painful sometimes, but like pain, it tells us that we are at risk, to be careful, to look after ourselves and to seek help.

Perhaps imposter syndrome does not signal our weakness or inadequacy; perhaps instead it reveals our courageousness for stepping into our future, not sinking into our past. When we are stretched, sometimes it will hurt.

People, like you, who have so much talent and so much potential, are not immune from doubt just because you are talented and have the potential to be wonderful, any more than an athlete is immune from pain at the limits of their exertion.

Our imposter syndrome is not something to hide from or fix, but to invite closer. When we feel it is close by, it is not there to undermine us, but as a witness to the moments that honour the gift of our potential. When it is with us, we are feeling what it is like to grow and to learn. Wisdom does not come from what we can do easily.

Perhaps the feelings we describe as fear or inadequacy are what it feels like to accumulate our wonderful, extraordinary and unique life story in real time.

Realising our potential is not a gentle slide into an easy listening paddling pool. It is to tumble in the waves of anxiety that accompany the absolute certainty we might fail. There are no imposters here, just brilliant people like you, doing amazing things as they realise that their hopes are ultimately bigger than their fears.

To deny the size of our challenges or the uncertainty our fears place upon us, is to deny our need for support and the size of our achievement when we succeed. We are all precious, powerful and beautifully vulnerable. When we ask for help, we empower others too. Then, when we succeed, it is real and shared.

Our fears are indeed powerful, however they are not there to shame us, but to show us that we are in the right place for our potential to shine.

The future of work ...and all that jazz

The existential questions come thick and fast.

They can be interesting and sometimes energising, but I am not always sure they help us. I think they mostly distract us. We end up, if we are not careful, daunted by a future we can hardly imagine, while we are stuck in a sub-optimal present that is all too familiar.

Take, for example the question "What is the future of work?"

I am not good at predicting the future, but I will have a stab at this one.

The future of work will still be full of imposed and often fatuous deadlines. Our work technology will always be mostly tired, utilitarian and more Trabant than Mercedes. Our priorities will often be determined by a desire to avoid conflict than the opportunity to make a difference.

Juxtapose this future, with all its familiar and muddily dysfunction, and then compare it with Linked-in which will reliably pop up several times a day with smiley exhortations for me to be TRANSFORMED by someone being implausibly energetic.

This is probably just me, but it is not the new ideas I object to and it is not that I am in a denial about how muddily and dysfunctional my present can be; it is the disconnect between the two that I cannot find a way to bridge. It means I do not see "transformation" as a good thing. I see it mostly as a threat, taking away the last hope I have of getting anything done at all. Like offering a drowning man lessons to learn the butterfly stroke while he is sinking. No, I do not want to learn a new swimming stroke, just throw me a bloody life belt or go away.

A breathless webinar may be wonderfully exciting to make, but please remember that you are now appearing in my home, with the full laundry basket just out of sight, the dog howling at the delivery man about to ring the doorbell, and not enough milk for my next cup of coffee.

I do not need your jazz-hands dashboard to help me understand how shit I am at getting through my to do list.

Then there is the most crushing line in all such webinars; the line when the host joyfully confirms that "if you have missed anything you can DOWNLOAD the content to watch it again".

(If I may digress for a moment, is there a more unattractive sounding idea than that of the "DOWNLOAD"? To "Down" "Load" – it doesn't exactly scream "Tiffany blue box" does it? Frankly short of calling something a "DUMPSPLASH", it really is quite the most unappealing idea for receiving anything from anyone at any time.)

So, it is the noise I struggle with. The hype, the hyperventilating and the disconnect with today that I resist. I know that my tech indifference (phobia) is not something to be proud of, but apart from email and Wi-Fi, I am struggling to think of any "tech" that has truly "transformed". The noise however does not abate, and so the future of work will be excitable combinations of agile, virtual, digital, atomised (fuck knows) and all manner of words which sooner or later will become another breathless webinar.

My concern therefore is not the tech, but with the fixation with the label and the hype. Legal Tech and Legal Ops is all very well, and I know is full of lovely people, but do we need them to be "TRANSFORMING"?

I would like them to be handy.

I would like them to be kind and valued; all of which would be great, and plenty.

I suspect these people are also mostly working on stuff that was not properly implemented by their predecessors. They are now living with the dawning realisation that the problem is not the idea, or the product, but the instances of everyday micro passive-aggressive resistance from everyone else who is just a little too busy, today, to listen, support or do anything even vaguely different.

It is, of course, hard to address such accumulated dysfunction, but for me it is not the answer for the evangelists to by-pass resistance with evermore hype. We are not far away now from legal tech being launched with sci-fi graphics, green screen animation and a whole cinematic backstory to play out on a dedicated You Tube channel presented by a teenage influencer with a billion followers because he once sucked porridge through a straw while setting fire to his eyebrows in his bedroom.

The future of work should not be hyped. Work is mostly useful, routine tasks that after a while bore the pants off us, spiced up with some Executive vanity initiative, plus buzzword bingo and the odd avoidable crisis to show we still have a functioning pulse between 9am and 6pm. The future of work is a boss who finds it hard to pretend anymore; an irritatingly aspirational junior who is unfeasibly happy to visit a supplier factory in Eastern Europe squished in the back of a 6am flight from Gatwick and who actually thinks it is developmental for their career. The future of work is also co-existing with several people who have seemingly retired from their roles but not yet persuaded HR to find a budget for them to leave the building. The future of work is, sadly, less about team building, and more about delaying the soul destroying. The future of work is now, and always will be, TOO MANY FUCKING EMAILS, jeesh!!!

The future of work is not meant to be designed, curated or innovative. It is meant to be A JOB where on a good day we rock up, are inoffensive, try to be kind, competent and present. We should care enough, but not too much; we should help where we can, but we should also realise that none of it really matters.

I do not mean to sound negative; I just want things to be in proportion. We can be more efficient by doing less, talking to each other more, and showing that we care more for the people than we do for the process.

Work tech does not make us happier; more often than not it is just better at counting how little difference we make to the pile of never-ending tasks our over-developed sense of duty encourages us to take on.

The future of work should be to ensure we have a better life outside of work. A place to love, laugh, cry, inspire, be inspired, run, sleep, walk, sit, drink tea, share, hug, touch, stare, smell, taste, rest and go again. Outside of work there is a future we should make time for and relish. Outside of work is where we should all want our best selves to be. The future of work is that it must do no harm.

Work is part of our lives. It should not matter more than that.

Hello silence, my old friend

The meeting room was full of noise.

Silence looked in, but she knew silence would not be welcome.

She therefore waited quietly outside just in case silence was needed.

She was happy to join the meeting at any time, but silence was never invited in.

It was such a shame; if only noise would remember that if a little silence is sprinkled around the words, then everyone can be heard. The mistake that noise always makes is thinking that silence is nothing; that silence does not matter; or that silence is weak and does not belong in a room full of noise.

Silence however is the extraordinary space where noise is decoded. Silence is the pause where understanding becomes possible. Silence brings meaning to our words, because silence knows that words which are unheard carry no meaning; they are just empty syllables, propelled on the turbulent winds of noise, lost forever in the tumble of sounds.

Silences create the unseen ephemeral network that connects us and our words and through which wisdom is revealed. This is how people learn from each other and grow; it is how goodness can flourish, and how kindness finds a place to serve.

The silence we give to ourselves is never empty and is never without its unsaid purpose. It holds a mirror to our intentions; it allows our thoughts to breathe and offers the light into which our hopes and ideas may emerge.

The silence we give to each other is our personal, thoughtful gift of grace. Such silence becomes the shape of our generosity and in its touch this silence shows how much we care. Silence is the gift of respect that feels at home in every culture and translates into any language. Silence offers equal opportunity, and highlights inequality. Silence lifts the vulnerable and mutes the powerful.

Silence perfectly placed in a conversation is an acknowledgement of power shared, of pain felt and joy honoured. Silence is the mark of our courage to listen and the acceptance of our need to be heard. Silence perfectly placed in a conversation is also the shelter for our own vulnerable thoughts and ideas; a harbour for our reflections and protection from the storm of louder voices.

For every leader, and every person who calls and manages a meeting, our responsibility above all is to ensure that silence is welcome in our meeting rooms. Such quiet moments, these pauses, allow us to perfectly curate where silence may land for people to be heard, and for purpose to be fulfilled.

Silence wrapped as a pause amplifies everyone's opportunity to be heard. In a world that can sometimes overwhelm us, or that can leave us feeling alone even in a crowded room, we make a powerful statement of a shared human experience when we offer to pause with each other. We all know how important this is because we all know how we feel when we are not heard.

It is never indulgent to listen, and it does not signal that we must agree, but the respect we show each other with silence offers opportunities for fresh insight, for understanding, for collaboration and for more secure and sustainable relationships.

Silence is a remarkable, free and replenishable resource. No budget is ever required for silence. When silence offers us so much, and asks so little of us in return, perhaps we should make more room for silence in our conversations and in our meetings.

Perhaps, as well, with silence to guide us, we might not need to use so many words.

And then perhaps the words we use might be chosen with more thought and care.

November 2020

It is not the answers we need most, but the courage to live without them

"Come in, sit down, I'll be with you in a moment, I'm just finishing a letter."

He stood framed by a bay window, his back to me, silhouetted against the morning light. He had a tape recorder in his hand and for the next minute and a half he dictated a client letter, punctuation included, a flat matter-of-fact tone, but calm, authoritative and certain. He put the recorder down and pulled his chair back to sit facing me across his immense desk. Towers of papers and files on either side of his pin-striped shoulders, his gold half-rimmed glasses low on his nose, he looked across the top of them and fixed his eyes on me.

"So, Paul, you want to be a solicitor; why?"

At that very moment, I seemed to lose the power of speech. Two seconds before I would have known the answer. I had rehearsed all manner of answers to all manner of questions; I was as well prepared for this moment of my life as I could possibly be, but just then I didn't have a relevant coherent syllable in my head.

I took a long, deep breath and paused for a few moments to notice what it was like to be in this room at this time. There were framed property deeds on the walls behind him, each with bright red seals like dollops of strawberry jam. There was an elegant lamp on his desk with a green glass shade. It offered little by way of light but illuminated a narrow strip of the leather inlay on his desk. Under my feet I could feel the runkle of a large ornate rug that made it hard to push back in my chair. I could see a family photograph of two smart looking boys in school uniform on top of a five-drawer black metal cabinet. One of the drawers was pulled out with a file open and resting on it. I could hear the tick-tock of a grandfather clock behind me, and I saw him take a sip of coffee from a white china cup.

I looked at the gentlemen opposite me, gathered in my anxiety and put it behind a smile, "Yes, I do want to be a solicitor; very much".

I really don't remember what I said next, but I must have said something reasonably sensible because a few days later I was offered a training contract. Later that year I started a journey that now brings me to a wet November morning in 2020 writing a blog post on my laptop about a conversation that happened in the summer of 1985.

As I write these words, I am amused by the quiet symmetrical bookends of thirty-five years of work in what I euphemistically call my career. It started with me watching a man in his late fifties dictating words into a handheld tape recorder, and now here I am, a man in my late fifties, tapping keys to create words on my computer. Both men comfortable with faded familiar things around them, and with a coffee within easy reach.

I am also struck by another, I hope more important, thought.

In 1985 I didn't know what might come next. I was frightened and I wasn't sure if I could cope with my new role, let alone succeed in it. I had no experience to call on and everything to come was unknown. Now in 2020 it is the same. I don't know what will come next. I am not sure if I will cope, let alone succeed, and this frightens me today as much as it did thirty-five years ago.

As our world is tipped upside down (again), so many things are unknown. However, the lad who took a deep breath in 1985 was about to start the adventure of his dreams. He was blessed to be helped by amazing people, to go to places he could not imagine and to have experiences (good and bad) that would enrich his life forever. Being frightened then was understandable and ok; and being frightened today is understandable and ok too.

We all have difficult days ahead, perhaps days that will be hard to face; but we have come this far. We have lived a bit, done things, felt things and achieved a great deal.

It is ok not to have all the answers today. Life's jagged journey is more often than not coming to terms with accepting that we're all looking for answers to something while trying to be comfortable with not knowing those answers or where to find them.

It is not the answers we need most, but the courage to live without them, the kindness of others to help us on our way and the openness to share what we have found to help others on their way too.

I still worry about the lad I was because he is always with me. His vulnerability was, and still is, real and constant, but he trusted that answers would come and that good people would look out for him too. Today I am certain that we will find our way again; and if we can be there for each other, we will work it out. We will be just fine.

Should we wear gardening clothes to work?

Dominic Cummings has, for now, left his role as the Prime Minister's controversial senior advisor.

Much will be written, a lot of it by Mr Cummings himself.

It may never be wholly clear* if his contribution to public life was a force for good, or just the predictable and self-destructive life cycle of another inadequate contrarian.

I think it is important however that we do not judge others without first knowing what it is like to walk in their shoes. I do not therefore judge Mr Cummings, but reflect instead on some of the things I believe to be true about me.

For example, if I were to write down one hundred "radical" ideas, I would hope that one or two of them might have a fighting chance of being interesting, perhaps of even happening one day. However, it would also be true that in no known universe would this make me a genius. Indisputably it would be fairer to say that I had written ninety-eight ideas that were well intended but in a range from not original, to dull, to embarrassingly shite.

If I were to wear my gardening clothes to work, when everyone else was expected to wear smart business attire, then in most people's eyes I would not be a troubled rebel, striking out against an overbearing dress code designed to inhibit my neurologically diverse thinking. It is much more likely to be the case that I am, in fact, an attention seeking arse.

If I have to criticise everyone around me who does not fit my world view, then I had better be right ALL of the time. For example, if we are tossing a coin, and if I call heads and heads it is, then my rightness is irrefutable. It may be irritating to be told "I told you it would be fucking heads, you fucking idiots" but you cannot argue with the result. However, if we are not tossing a coin, but instead (let's say) embarking upon the most economically significant and geo-politically divisive event of our lifetimes, then it might be nice to see a little evidence of the upside to help everyone accept my idiosyncratic and expletive filled determination to change the world.

On a similar point, if I had been tempted to splash a little paint on the side of a bus to describe one of my two really cool radical ideas, I might also have worked on an inclusive, well-crafted and comprehensive implementation strategy to answer the all too predictable follow up question.

And perhaps, if I were to suddenly walk away from a mess that I had helped create, I would not expect to be seen as the personification of tragic, misunderstood ennui, as I walk from my office, holding a cardboard box of metaphorical pathos. I think it more likely that I would be seen as a truculent knobhead.

I realise I am describing myself in these points, and it is unfair to extrapolate more widely, but there could be wider truths in such reflections.

Could it possibly be, for example, that if we over-rely on an idea and forget the importance of being kind, generous, thoughtful, considerate and patient, we might not make as much progress as we would like to make?

Could it be, for example, that if we invest in our own image at the expense of how other people feel around us, then when we need those people to step in for us, they might all have taken a step away?

And could it be that if we constantly promote a sense of our own infallibility, that no-one will give a flying saucepan lid when we become predictably fallible.

*it is pretty clear.

We're not the same, but we get to carry each other

An animated conversation between friends about our favourite bands is often a joyful distraction revealing our long lost teenage tribes.

It can also mean stepping into perilous conversations about fashion, big hair and album covers. I am not saying that leg warmers and 80's power ballads are not culturally significant (obviously!) and all of this deserves several glasses of inexpensive Chardonnay to fuel the debate. However, if instead we were to talk about the song lyrics that made us pause, the conversation might change from one that requires us to open a bottle, to one that opens a small window for the gentleness of fresh air on old feelings.

A song that has always paused my spinning mind in the past, and does so even more today, is U2's One; it opens with these lines:

"Is it getting better
Or do you feel the same
Will it make it easier on you now
You got someone to blame"

What I am about to write I do not say lightly, and not for effect. Neither do I want to underplay my anxiety or anyone's pain. We all need support, time to heal and time to grow, but if we have one love and we can use it every day, what would be the downside of showing that we care? If we have one love, why would we not use it? Does it not say who we are far more than the trappings of apparent success or apparent failure?

In some respects, this year has been the most difficult year of my career. A business that took nineteen years to build has quietly disappeared in a few months. A business as a balance sheet is an ice sculpture that can melt in front of your eyes.

But of course, this is not the whole picture.

My work is not defined by a set of forms filed at Companies House, or a share certificate or even a brand. My work is the difference we have made to those who have trusted our care. It is the way we try to touch minds, to touch hearts and it is the means for us to celebrate the potential or our clients and delegates to be extraordinary.

A balance sheet is a record of value in only one dimension. However, I can (and do) reflect on all the opportunities our business gives me to see value in so many different dimensions at the same time. This does not diminish the disappointment and pain of loss, but neither does it reduce the joy and diversity of relationships, experiences and emotions. I know that the difference we make is not captured in the cells of an Excel spreadsheet.

Of course, 2020 has not been easy, to say the least, but it has been rich in gifts of reflection, kindness, generosity and care. It has been the year we learned again the power of love to carry each other.

So, when I think of this song, I know that I have one love and I know that things will get better again, but I also know that it doesn't get easier because you have someone else to blame. Blame would be a distraction, a place to shrink and hide. Blame is an energy I don't have the time or the desire to ride.

As we face this winter of our disconnect from the people and things we love, it is ok to be disappointed, to be frightened, and to feel exhausted by it all. It is perfectly understandable if we feel all of this viscerally; but even then, we are so much more than these things alone. Even in the dark we can still smile, we can still love, care, share, and ask each other if we are ok.

We may feel that our potential to make a difference is defined by our roles, or job titles; or will be constrained if we find ourselves between roles for now. However, our potential to be extraordinary is revealed in every thoughtful gift of kindness and care, it is not defined by a balance sheet, or another person's decision that our role must change or be lost. We have one love, and we can use it however we want. No budget is required, no status is required, and no permission is required to care. Our one love is always with us, and is always for us...

"...we're not the same but we get to carry each other, carry each other. One love."

December 2020

This will be over...

This will be over.

And we will know when.

It will be over when we can meet again in our favourite place for coffee, searching for a table that isn't the one next to the open door, or the loud guy on his phone.

When we can knock a pub table with our knee and, with open mouths in freeze-frame, wait for the fate of the brim-full drinks we have just placed so carefully in front of our friends.

When we can love talking over each other's sentences and delight in the murmuration of conversation as overlapping words take flight.

When we notice the rising hubbub of a room that is full of expectation and thinking out loud, like an orchestra warming up before the symphony begins.

And when such a room can be brought to silence simply by clinking the side of a small glass.

When a slightly raised eyebrow says it all.

When we can laugh again and not have to explain.

When we can include knowing looks in our repertoire of feedback.

And if we notice that someone might not be feeling their best, the briefest touch of their arm is the gentlest means to connect.

When we do not have to take a deep breath before pressing the link for the umpteenth video call of the day, or feel the pressure to be Zoom cheerful because our concerns are not as great as the concerns that others must have.

When we are distracted by a conversation nearby that we cannot quite hear, but delight in the art and the joy of surreptitious listening.

When bumping into a colleague we have not seen for a while lights up the corridor with smiles and the fast exchange of family news.

When an unexpected shower of rain catches us without a coat and, as we drip through a marbled reception, we hope our hair suggests art-house perfume advertisement, rather more than cockerpoo for-fucks-sake-bedraggled.

When we arrive early for an appointment and can relish the quiet oasis of a few minutes with our undisturbed thoughts; and then notice the peace that comes when we can do nothing but wait.

When a stranger's smile can make our day.

When opening a door for someone adds a drop of kindness into the world that was not there before.

When we can leave a meeting room feeling we have nailed all the points we wanted to make and someone who was there, passes us by and whispers "well done".

When we can dash for a train we should have left more time to catch, and allow the thought to live on our smile that we are in a Bourne film escaping the crescendo of a sweeping orchestral score.

When getting home is the best safe feeling in the world and we wonder what stories we will tell and what stories we will hear.

When a hug is what happens to acknowledge the joy of connection and not the sadness of loss.

When this wretched year is a memory that we can use to help each other cope a little better with whatever future travails and injustices will inevitably come our way.

When we can reflect that we have coped damn well and be proud that all our stories matter.

When we can say out loud that this is ok, and then notice that being ok is all we ever really wanted.

When saying "I love you" is a vessel of hope for joys to come as much as it is a life raft for joys past.

This will be over.

And we will know when.

Until then please take the greatest care.

Other books by Paul

All these books can be bought from the
LBC Wise Counsel website: **www.lbcwisecounsel.com**

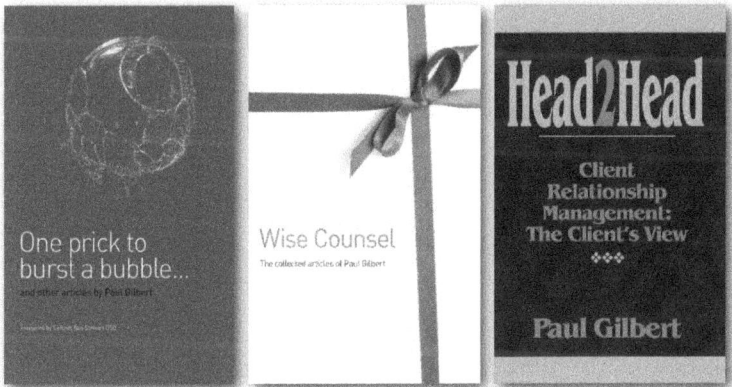